6 books in 1

HTeBooks

Copyright © 2016

Copyright © 2016 HTeBooks

All rights reserved. This book or any portion thereof may not be reproduced or used in any manner whatsoever without the express written permission of the publisher except for the use of brief quotations in a book review.

Disclaimer

This book is designed to provide condensed information. It is not intended to reprint all the information that is otherwise available, but instead to complement, amplify and supplement other texts. You are urged to read all the available material, learn as much as possible and tailor the information to your individual needs.

Every effort has been made to make this book as complete and as accurate as possible. However, there may be mistakes, both typographical and in content. Therefore, this text should be used only as a general guide and not as the ultimate source of information. The purpose of this book is to educate.

The author or the publisher shall have neither liability nor responsibility to any person or entity regarding any loss or damage caused, or alleged to have been caused, directly or indirectly, by the information contained in this book.

Book List

HOW TO BECOME A LEARNING MACHINE 4

HOW TO BECOME A MEMORY MASTER 32

HOW TO BOOST YOUR CREATIVITY 60

HOW TO FIND YOUR TALENTS AND STRENGTHS 86

HOW TO LEARN ANY LANGUAGE FAST 114

HOW TO LEARN ANY SKILL FAST 144

How To Become a Learning Machine

This book aims to help one become a learning machine by defining what learning is, acknowledging the importance of learning and identifying and prevailing over the factors affecting it to promote learning in all aspects by increasing knowledge, cultivating skills and attaining wisdom.

> "The illiterate of the 21st century will not be those who cannot read and write, but those who cannot learn, unlearn, and relearn."
>
> - Alvin Toffler

What is Learning?

"All our knowledge begins with the senses, then proceeds to the understanding and ends with reason. There is nothing higher than reason."
                                    - Immanuel Kant

Learning is defined as the act or process of gaining new knowledge, skills and attitudes or modifying or strengthening existing ones and integrating them as may be deemed useful to achieve one's goals.

Learning as a Process

Learning is not completed at one single time. It does not simply involve receiving information. It is a continuous process that is undergone by every individual who uses his reason to take in information and arrange them in such a way that they become understandable and useful.

Gaining New Knowledge, Skills and Attitudes

Knowledge, skills and attitudes may be acquired in various ways: through reading, observation, experience and teaching. Reading enables one to learn something through someone else's documented testimony or evidence of a subject he sought to explain through investigation, research or even experience. Observation enables the acquisition of personal knowledge about certain matters. Experience enables the acquisition of knowledge which may or may not have been taught. It is particularly important in learning skills, which must indeed be practiced to be learned. Knowledge acquired from being taught may be either enlightened or corruptible. Enlightened knowledge refers to that which requires explanation to be understood such as mathematical or scientific principles. On the other hand, corruptible knowledge refers to that which may be tainted with the teacher's biases upon being taught such as history and theology.

Modifying and Strengthening Existing Knowledge, Skills and Attitudes

Learning enables one to modify or strengthen his existing knowledge, skills and attitudes when he acknowledges and accepts new developments or revisions to that which he already knows. In simpler terms, this is what is known as adapting. It is particularly useful in finding better solutions to problems. An example of this is the development of vaccines to avoid being infected or afflicted with a serious illness.

Integrating

Finally, the key to learning lies in integration. Integration involves synthesizing all the information acquired through time and evaluating how they have been used in history or how they can be applied in a particular situation at present or even in the future.

In other words, integration entails the use of reason. Reason is defined as the ability to make sense of the information at hand by relating ideas to one another and understanding them with cause and effect (consequence), fact or fiction (truth) and good or bad (morality). It requires a conscious effort of validating facts and applying logic to justify or change existing beliefs and practices.

*Learning entails the use of reason.

The Importance of Learning

"Learning is the only thing the mind never exhausts, never fears, and never regrets."

- Leonardo da Vinci

Since the dawn of time, life has posed many challenges for man—from the allocation of limited resources and fear of the unknown to the consequences of failure. However, civilization continues to thrive as man persists in enduring and overcoming them by using the innate ability of his mind to learn.

Learning starts even before an individual is ready to go to school. While children and even babies are known to display an interest in learning, studies conducted within the latest decade have shown that an individual's motivation for learning declines upon reaching his teens. In fact, data from the National Research Council reveals that more than 40 per cent of high school students are constantly absent or withdrawn from school due to lack of motivation.

Nevertheless, such a condition is subject to change over time as research shows that more than 90 per cent of adults are more motivated to learn with various personal reasons such as to get a better paying job, boosting confidence, improving the quality of life and satisfaction.

While such reasons may encourage one's desire to learn, the importance of learning is simply that it allows individuals to freely stretch the limits of their humanity to find answers to their questions.

In other words, the universal and primary importance of learning is that through it, man is able to fulfill his essence as a thinking being and nothing can be greater than that.

*Learning is important because it enables man to fulfill his essence as a thinking being.

Factors Affecting Learning and how to Prevail Over Them

"The knowledge of all things is possible."

- Leonardo da Vinci

It is possible for man to know or learn everything he wants. However, learning is not easy. It may be affected by internal and external factors which must be dealt with so that true learning may ensue.

Internal Factors

Internal factors are those which originate from the individual's genetic make-up and intelligence. More specifically, it consists of his capacity to learn, his attitude towards learning and his motivation.

Capacity to Learn and Attitude towards Learning

An individual's capacity to learn and attitude towards learning often go hand in hand. While an individual's capacity to learn may be affected by his physical condition or traits, innate talent and intellect, the lack thereof does not necessarily preclude him from learning. It also doesn't mean that just because an individual is born with talent, he should not continue to learn to improve his craft. This is where an individual's attitude towards learning plays an important role. A major component of this attitude towards learning is having strength of will. If he is determined to learn and persists in doing so in spite of all the odds against him, then he shall most likely become a genius in his own right.

For instance, in spite of his musical talents, German composer and pianist Ludwig van Beethoven devoted his time to studying and learning under the direction of Classical composer Franz Joseph Haydn before setting out to become a composer. Although he became deaf by the age of 26, he was yet able to continue producing great works such as his famous masterpiece, The Ninth Symphony.

Similarly, American author Helen Keller, who became deaf and blind due to an illness before reaching the age of two, persisted in learning until she graduated cum laude with her Bachelor of Arts degree in Radcliffe College. In spite of her physical disabilities, she was also able to write several essays and twelve books which were eventually published.

On a different note, contrary to the impression his fans have of him, basketball star Michael Jordan likewise had to learn how to perfect his jump shot to become a legend in spite of his phenomenal athletic skills and complementary physical attributes, as revealed by his longstanding coach, Phil Jackson.

Another component of an individual's attitude towards learning also requires him to have an open mind. This involves challenging ideas before accepting them and accepting them only if they have not yet been displaced by new discoveries or innovative ideas.

An example of this—though considered controversial in other places around the world--is learning without any religious biases. It is difficult to learn many things about life in general if one has to start with the assumption that everything comes from God. Another example is the acceptance of the flat earth model which was held from the classical to the Hellenistic periods until a new idea of the Earth as a sphere emerged with Pythagoras until it was proven by Christopher Columbus in his voyage around the earth.

Motivation

Unless a person acknowledges and accepts his essence as a thinking being as the primary motivation for learning, he is only capable of obtaining provisional knowledge which can fade through time after the particular motivation for learning has been attained. Accepting one's essence as a thinking being enables the pursuit of true learning: learning for learning's sake.

External Factors

External factors are those which are usually beyond the control of the individual. They include the availability of resources, the source of learning, the cost of learning and the environmental conditions.

Availability of Resources

In reality, everything can be considered a resource for learning. However, the availability of resources for specific learning may be limited and quite costly. For instance, the individual's financial resources may not be sufficient to cover the cost of learning a particular course like Law which requires paying fees for enrollment in college and subsequently, Law School including the cost of materials such as law books and other incidental fees like transportation and lodging which can reach a minimum of approximately $30,000 to a maximum of more than $80,000 and may vary according to state.

Nevertheless, the lack of resources must not serve as an obstacle for individuals who truly want to learn as other options may be available. For instance, Abraham Lincoln, the 16th President of the United States, learned the law and became a lawyer without going to law school. He studied the law independently and obtained his license to practice law after passing an oral examination in front of a panel of lawyers in the Sangamon Country Court, Illinois. Although circumstances may have become more difficult in the past few decades, options for learning to become a lawyer are still available particularly in the states of Wyoming, California, Virginia, Vermont and Washington where self-study of the law together with apprenticeship can qualify an individual for the BAR exams and eventually practice law as an attorney.

Another valuable resource which people often fail to consider is time. It is limited to the present because the past no longer exists and the future is always unknown. Thus, an individual who wishes to learn must start now and even if the future holds no certainty, he may still set a reasonable time for everything he wants to learn. After all, time is only consumed in so far as events transpired before the present. The future still holds possibilities.

Source of Learning

One factor that affects the quality of learning is its source. It can either encourage true learning or serve as a hindrance to it. This is particularly true for subjects which are taught without the need for presenting empirical evidence. For instance, the lessons of history can be tainted with the teacher's ideological biases which can influence the students' minds. True learning is best obtained from firsthand experience or authoritative documentation such as books, academic journals or published texts by specialists on the given subject. On the other hand, true learning is impeded when one merely relies on opinionated articles or readily available or secondhand information particularly in the internet such as Wikipedia. In the words of the great Roman philosopher Marcus Tullius Cicero himself, "The authority of those who teach is often an obstacle to those who want to learn."

Environment

The environment largely contributes to an individual's ability to learn. It consists of the areas in which he moves such as the home, school and neighborhood as well as the city, state or country where he belongs.

Home

The home is one's primary place of learning. From his earliest motor and cognitive skills to his first interpersonal relationships as well as academic pursuits, the home has served as his first school. Thus, an atmosphere conducive for learning must be maintained always. This includes the encouragement and support of family members, the neatness and orderliness of study areas as well as freedom from noise and other distractions.

School

An individual usually pursues more specific areas of study in school. It can inspire him to pursue higher learning or discourage him from further learning depending on the following elements: teaching style, system of assessment, extracurricular activities and pressure groups.

Teaching Style

Teaching style can greatly affect an individual's learning as it refers to the manner in which lessons are taught. Studies have shown that interactive teaching styles are more effective than traditional information transfer through lectures as they produce better understanding and higher grades.

System of Assessment

Grades are based on the system of assessment which may vary for every teacher. However, subjective criteria for evaluation should be avoided to measure actual learning with more accuracy. Moreover, the system of assessment must also be able to measure how much the student has learned and not just provide a basis for grades. In other words, tests must be formulated to generate critical thinking based on the given information while projects and other requirements must be an application of relevant theories, principles or ideas. For instance, history tests must not consist solely of identification of names and dates but more importantly, of reasons, causes and effects. Similarly, math and science projects should present more challenges by encouraging new ideas in the application of mathematical and scientific knowledge.

Extracurricular Activities

Learning is not limited to the intellect. The existence of extracurricular activities such as intramurals, school fairs, dances, homecomings, competitions and other organizations encourages an individual's complete learning as he is allowed to explore other aspects of his being.

Pressure groups

While the presence of pressure groups such as bullies, junkies, frat men, sorority girls, racists or snooty cliques can discourage an individual from learning in school, they can, on the other hand, serve as competition and push the strong-willed to learn more or serve as subjects to individuals who want to learn about human behavior.

Neighborhood

An individual's neighborhood can either function as his prison cell or his laboratory, depending on his desire to learn. For instance, a neighborhood run by goons or drug dealers can prevent him from exploring his surroundings due to the threats he may come across. On the other hand, a peaceful and secure neighborhood can function as his laboratory where he is free to explore his surroundings and interact with his neighbors healthily.

City, State or Country

Finally, an individual's learning can also be affected by the larger area where he belongs. More specifically, some cities have strict regulations such as zoning laws which may prohibit certain activities on particular lots while some countries which continue to discriminate against race and gender prohibit the education of certain groups. For instance, in Middle Eastern countries like Kuwait and Oman, education is biased in favor of male in students as female students are required to obtain higher averages to be able admitted in certain courses like engineering as well as in Saudi Arabia where more classes and courses are made available to men than to women.

Democratic countries such as the United States, on the other hand, provide greater learning opportunities for all through government-funded scholarships, grants and other incentives. Similarly, companies and non-governmental institutions create educational opportunities as well.

Considerably, nothing can prevent an individual from learning except himself.

Prevailing over these factors will enable him to pursue true learning by increasing his knowledge, cultivating his skills and attaining wisdom.

*The propensity to overcome obstacles is directly proportional to one's desire for learning.

Increasing Knowledge

"To know what you know and what you do not know, that is true knowledge."

- Confucius

Knowledge is defined as information consisting of facts or theories pertaining to a certain subject. In a more general context, it is the sum of all truths and principles acquired and accumulated through time and upheld by humanity. It may pertain to truths which must yet be established or those which have already been ascertained or at least, have been accepted as true.

Learning truths which must yet be established

There are two ways of generating knowledge which remains to be established: through rationalism and empiricism. Rationalism makes use of innate ideas, logic and deductive reasoning which relies on premises to arrive at a definite conclusion. On the other hand, empiricism involves the use of observation and inductive reasoning which only requires strong evidence instead of absolute proof as the basis for the conclusion.

Knowledge through Rationalism

Rationalism presupposes that man is born with innate ideas which, according to philosophers like Plato, can explain why some individuals are naturally better at performing or resolving some tasks than others are in spite of the similarity of experiences. It also acknowledges reason as the major cause of knowledge in contrast with the senses which, according to rationalists like Descartes, can only give opinions since they can be deceived. Thus, conclusions can be proven with certainty using rationalism. An example of this is Descarte's attempt to prove the existence of God where he starts with the premise that he has an idea of a perfect substance but since he is not a perfect substance, a perfect substance like God must exist because only perfection is capable of creating perfection.

Knowledge through Empiricism

Empiricism, on the other hand, presumes that knowledge originates from perception. More specifically, philosopher John Locke explains that simple ideas are based on perception or observation of physical qualities like shape or color while complex ideas are formed by combining simple ideas. Empiricists reject innate ideas as the source of knowledge because individuals do not demonstrate knowledge at birth or in the early stages of their life as in childhood, where children must learn how to talk and walk. Thus, empiricists believe that things cannot be proven conclusively as no one can be certain that the thing remains the same once the individual stops perceiving it. In other words, the mind is likened to a blank slate upon which experience imparts knowledge in all aspects—intelligence, social and emotional behavior.

Debating on their acceptability is quite useless since there is absolutely no conflict as both ways can be applied in learning. Rationalism may be used to learn about things which observation cannot answer such as the existence of God while empiricism may be used to learn about things which must rely on observation to be applied effectively as in scientific studies on the effects of medicine, etc.

Learning truths which have already been ascertained or accepted as true

Rationalism and empiricism are generally used in obtaining knowledge which has not yet been accepted as true. However, for facts which have already been ascertained or accepted as true, one may employ one or more learning styles to aid in his absorption of knowledge. These learning styles can be generally divided into two: individual or social learning.

Individual learning

Individual learning style presumes one's preference for self-study. The desire to work alone usually enables one to learn at his ideal pace and align learning objectives with personal values and standards.

Individual learning further enables one to choose freely among the following learning styles to suit his needs: visual learning, auditory learning, physical learning and logical or mathematical learning.

Visual learning

This learning style generally starts with looking at an entire system, the whole or the "big picture" before probing into the details. It makes use of images such as photos, drawings or other visual aids like tables, graphs and charts instead of words in learning. It may also use imagination or photographic memory and color-coding of notes. This style is recommended for learning how to write foreign words which require the use of characters such as Chinese, Japanese or Korean, memorizing geographic locations and descriptions or legal cases involving family relations or crime.

Auditory Learning

Auditory learning makes use of any kind of sound whether used as a background for studying or to facilitate association or recall. For instance, using classical music, particularly that of Mozart as a background for studying, has been shown in studies conducted at Stanford University to have beneficial effects including the reduction of learning time, the decrease in errors and the improvement of clarity. On the other hand, association and recall of information may be enhanced by developing them into rhymes or incorporating them in rhythmic beats and popular jingles. This also includes recording one's voice or orally repeating important points which can help strengthen memory. This type of learning is particularly useful for learning how to speak a foreign language.

Physical learning

Physical learning entails field work or active participation by making use of physical objects to help demonstrate theories which may be difficult to understand. For instance, using common tools like a nutcracker or tweezers to demonstrate laws of physics may help in understanding terms such as effort, fulcrum and resistance more easily. Similarly, toys like cubes and balls or origami creations may also be used to explain geometric theories like lines, planes, spheres and space. It may also mean learning while doing a physical activity such as jogging, going back and forth across the room or eating.

Logical or Mathematical Learning

Logical or mathematical learning generally entails using specific principles in the mathematical system to understand how formulas were derived to be able to solve mathematical problems more easily in contrast to memorization without reason, which can produce disastrous results if there is a mental block. An example would be using theorems to prove congruence in geometry and properties of multiplication, addition and equality to solve for unknown variables in algebra.

Social Learning

This type of learning is for individuals who prefer to learn from others in groups through activities like sharing, role playing, constructive argumentation or debates.

With all the learning styles available, man has no excuse to remain ignorant.

*There are many ways to gain knowledge.

Cultivating Skills

"For the things we have to learn before we can do them, we learn by doing them."

- Aristotle

To become a learning genius, one must not confine himself to the pursuit of knowledge. Whether born as or developed into, geniuses are exceptional at different forms of learning. As shown in the previous chapter, they can successfully use their reason to discover new knowledge or modify accepted truths. In terms of skills, learning geniuses can either discover and unleash their skills or establish themselves as creative geniuses in the performance of their skills.

A skill is defined as the ability to perform physical tasks with a certain degree of aptitude. They may either be general or specific.

General Skills

General skills are those which are transferrable or applicable to various activities or functions in all sectors—whether household, commercial or financial, industrial, educational or social. They include leadership, organization, budget administration, time management and communication.

Specific Skills

Specific skills, on the other hand, are those which are functional or effective only for a particular task such as auditing skills for an accountant, culinary skills for a chef or hair cutting and coloring skills for hairdressers.

Like knowledge, skills may either be learned or enhanced. In both cases, training, practice and persistence are required.

Training

Training is defined as the process of acquiring certain competencies from professionals or experts in order to achieve a higher standard of proficiency. It may be undertaken through formal lessons for talents such as singing, dancing and playing the piano or apprenticeships for technical skills for electricians and auto mechanics.

Practice

Practice entails the repeated performance of specific exercises designed to increase proficiency. In order to obtain the best results, one must first take note of his mistakes and avoid committing them again. Moreover, he must not reduce the act of rehearsing into a mere routine. Instead, he must perform passionately and seek to surpass each performance with a challenge to go beyond perfection. After all, one can find himself in losing himself.

Persistence

Persistence is a quality which enables one to continue doing something in spite of some difficulties he may encounter. For instance, although Van Gogh began drawing in his childhood until he decided to become an artist, he produced a multitude of sketches in order to improve his talent for years before he finally completed his best art works in the remaining years of his life. Although it took more than a decade for his works to be recognized, he continued to strive for perfection.

Similarly, four-time Grammy Award winner Taylor Swift, who started writing songs when she was five, persisted in writing and singing her music in spite of being mistreated by fellow students in school and unfairly judged by critics until she was finally recognized by Sony Music publishing and became the star that she is.

Talent without persistence can go unrecognized.

*One can be born with talent and skill but it is in persistence that he can achieve greatness.

Attaining Wisdom

"Wisdom is not a product of schooling but of the lifelong attempt to acquire it."

- Albert Einstein

More than knowledge and skills, the ultimate goal of a learning genius is to acquire wisdom. Wisdom is defined as the ability to incorporate knowledge, awareness, experience, retrospection and understanding in order to act or make a choice. As such, it cannot be taught or learned in school. It is the result of one's assessment of his experiences where he recognizes his mistakes and resolves to avoid them in future instances.

It requires knowledge relevant to the given situation in order to evaluate his predicament and determine what can be done, awareness of what he is faced with (resources, alternatives and advantages or disadvantages), experience and retrospection in order to enable him to make the right judgment and understanding in order to be able to deal with the possible consequences of his choice. In other words, it is knowing exactly what to say or do in any given situation and being ready to accept the consequences of one's actions.

Thus, wisdom has four components: the ability to accept the limits of one's knowledge, the ability to find the middle ground, the ability to exercise objectivity and the ability to apply foresight.

Accepting the limits of one's knowledge

In order to make a good decision, one must turn to his own knowledge involving the issue at hand. However, he must learn to admit when his knowledge is insufficient to allow him to make the correct decision. In such cases, he may either refer to other sources or seek counsel from qualified authorities before making a decision.

Finding the Middle Ground

Finding the middle ground entails the ability to compromise. It involves reaching an agreement where all parties forfeit individual benefits in favor of a mutually advantageous arrangement. This is particularly useful in situations requiring negotiations such as collective bargaining agreements, business transactions or even a hostage crisis.

Exercising Objectivity

In order to arrive at a compromise, one must necessarily exercise objectivity and weigh all matters from each party's respective standpoints. It is only by doing so that a mutually beneficial arrangement can be reached. Furthermore, objectivity enables one to think clearly and use his reason more effectively as it will not be clouded with subjective biases. This is best exemplified in judicial pronouncements of acquittal or conviction as well as matters pertaining to morality.

Applying Foresight

Foresight is the ability to foresee all possible outcomes of a certain course of action. It allows the individual to choose the best course of action out of all possible actions and enables him to accept the consequences that may arise therefrom, knowing that the outcome was the least disadvantageous result among the only courses of action available at that time. This may be applied in times of financial crisis when one is faced with various alternatives for producing funds. For instance, choosing to sell one's assets instead of contracting an interest-generating loan would be the less disadvantageous for the individual as his liabilities will not increase.

All in all, wisdom guides man in all his judgments. Thus, it is the greatest purpose of learning.

*The attainment of wisdom is the ultimate goal of learning.

Become a Learning Genius

"Change is the end result of all true learning."

- Leo Buscaglia

While one might argue that there are truths which cannot be changed like the law of gravity or that a routinely life does not enable the discovery of anything new, everyone nevertheless learns something new everyday. This is because everyday is a different day. It is not yesterday.

A learning genius never runs out of things to learn for he knows that there are still other things which he does not know and what he knows today might not be the same tomorrow or if not, after an extended period of time. For instance, the geocentric model of the universe espoused by philosophers like Aristotle and Ptolemy which ancient civilizations accepted as true for hundreds of years was later on replaced with the model of heliocentrism as advocated by Nicolaus Copernicus, Galileo Galilei and Johannes Kepler, which did not become popular until the 16th century.

Similarly, the theory of spontaneous generation promoted by philosophers like Anaximander, Hippolytus, Aristotle and Anaxagoras which provides that life could be produced from nothing (as in the case of maggots coming out of biodegradable objects like animal carcasses or rotting fruit) was generally held as true for centuries and was proven wrong only after the 1700s with the use of the scientific method where such theories were tested. More specifically, they were immediately proven wrong when microbiologist Louis Pasteur used experimentation to show that maggots did not appear on meat which was sealed in a container and were instead produced by airborne microorganisms as seen through the microscope which was newly invented at that time. To wit, new inventions and further experimentation can lead to new learning which can refute and modify existing truths.

As long as there is life, everyone continues to learn by observation and by experience. Some choose to continue to improve their skills and strive to be better than yesterday while some choose to give up. Nevertheless, each choice made by an individual is a learning opportunity for another. Every question generates an answer and each answer is a new learning for the inquisitive mind. Only the mind can challenge what it already knows.

*A learning genius, therefore, never ceases to use his reason in all things, at all times.

How to Apply What You've Learned?

*Learning entails the use of reason.

*Learning is important because it enables man to fulfill his essence as a thinking being.

*The propensity to overcome obstacles is directly proportional to one's desire for learning.

*There are many ways to gain knowledge.

*One can be born with talent and skill but it is in persistence that he can achieve greatness.

*The attainment of wisdom is the ultimate goal of learning.

*A learning genius, therefore, never ceases to use his reason in all things, at all times.

How To Become a Memory Master

Memory decline is a normal and natural part of the aging process. You will experience it whether you like it or not because your brain ages as your body does. Likewise, you will experience some difficulty recalling things at some point because your mental health is closely linked to your emotional and physical health. Needless to say, everyone has his or her own share of ups and downs. A simple case of stress or severe case of depression can both lead to memory decline, albeit usually, only temporarily.

The concern here is not really to stop memory decline, but to delay it and alleviate the changes to as mild as possible. Many older people past the age of 80and still have clear memories because they have successfully delayed their mental aging through mental exercises, healthy lifestyle, and optimum support. All of this will be discussed in this book.

You will grow old but you can refuse to get rusty. This book aims to show you the proven ways to stop memory loss altogether and maintain your sharp memory all your life. You might experience some stumbles one time or another, as with anybody else, but the important thing is you become consistent with your mental performance.

Simple Tricks for a Failing Memory

"The sense of smell can be extraordinarily evocative, bringing back pictures as sharp as photographs of scenes that had left the conscious mind."

- Thalassa Cruso

Sometimes, the key to thinking harder when trying to recall something is not overthinking it. There are quick tricks you can do whenever your memory is failing you. These tricks will help you if you need a quick mental fix.

1. Sniff rosemary and lavender fragrance

Aromatherapy is a homeopathic solution to failing memory. Specifically, rosemary and lavender have shown promise in enhancing memory by stimulating the brain, especially when sniffed or when you are trying to recall something. Instead of going for the fruity scents, use these fragrances in the form of diluted oil, potpourri, candle, or even air freshener.

2. Move your eyes left and right

Moving your eyes left and right whenever you are trying to recall something, such as a term or formula, can help you trigger your memory because by doing so, you are realigning the two regions of your brain to make them work harder. You can do this trick even when not trying to recall something, like every morning as a part of your mental preparation for the whole day.

3. Move your eyes to the left

Moving your eyes to the left several times when trying to recall an idea you have created, such as a storyline or plot, can help you trigger your memory because the left side of your brain is dedicated to your creativity. You can do this trick when writing or talking about your ideas. Just avoid doing it when in an interview because the interviewer, who probably has a background in psychology, might think that you are making up stories.

4. Move your eyes to the right

Moving your eyes to the right several times when trying to recall a formula (any mathematical operation for that matter) or reason out will help you because the right part of your brain is in charge of math and reasoning.

5. Read words aloud when memorizing

When you memorize, you chiefly use your eyes to record words or pictures, while you rely on your visualization skills to recall things that you have memorized before but do not naturally pop into your head (like the name of a person familiar to you but you do not necessary call by name everyday). You are practically tapping just a single sense. By using another one, you are getting a reinforcement to make memorization easier and recalling faster.

To do this, read aloud the words you are memorizing, so your auditory sense is also activated. If you are memorizing a speech or presentation, read it to yourself over and over again, so your brain also records the spoken words aside from the printed words.

Key Points/Action Steps:

*)Do not fret when recalling seems too hard at times. You need to keep cool and just do the tricks shared in this chapter.

*)Do these tricks even when you are not having a hard time recalling. They will serve as your exercise to help you in the long run.

*)Forgetting something is not absolute on normal cases. Your memory is definitely improvable.

Improving Memory with a Healthy Lifestyle

"Own only what you can always carry with you: know languages, know countries, know people. Let your memory be your travel bag."

- Aleksandr Solzhenitsyn

Living a healthy lifestyle will help you live a fuller life, free of blank pages in your head. The brain is connected to your body and so what you do to your body happens to your brain. You have to love and take care of yourself if you want your brain to reciprocate with good memories. You might not feel any changes now with regard to your mental performance, but sooner or later, if you will not change your bad habits, you will suffer an early onset of age-related memory decline.

Here are some tips to maintain a healthy lifestyle.

1. Go out more often

How can you improve your memory if you do not have much valuable ones to recall to begin with? As your brain deletes short-term memories and stores long-term ones, you also need to feed it with new ones constantly to keep it building and working out. You have to stimulate your imagination with real images and sensations. You also have to learn new things to reinforce old memories.

Experience is the best teacher, and it can be the best memory booster as well.

2. Sleep early and enough

If you don't feel tired even if you only got a couple of hours', sleep does not mean everything is fine. Usually, your brain suffers what your body cannot feel. As you deprive yourself of proper sleep, your brain's function also starts to wane considerably, but the long-term effect probably won't be apparent until you hit your senior years.

Your sleep time is your brain's chance to fix everything that needs fixing. It deletes short-term memories and reinforces long-term memories. This is the time when your brain connects related information together and stimulates the production of new neurons that will keep the passage of data active.

According to the journal *Sleep Medicine*, insufficient sleep of less than eight hours a day will lead to slower cognitive ability, less mental concentration, and faster mental exhaustion.

3. Take a rest when mentally tired

Students like to spend the whole night reviewing past lessons during their exam weeks. Employees like to work nonstop to get the job done the fastest way possible. Most people want to push their mental capacities just to get their tasks done without actually considering the risk of getting bad results with poor mental performance.

The brain is responsible for the 20% of your entire daily calorie consumption. Just imagine how much workout your brain actually does in a day. That is tiring.

When you push your brain too hard, you are actually damaging it by encouraging more deletion of memories than storage. The brain does this to lessen the burden it experiences from trying to recall so many bits of information even if you do not have sufficient energy to do so.

You won't be able to think clearly if you are mentally and physically tired, so better reserve your energy for another time.

Key Points/Action Steps:

*)**Your brain is like muscles; it needs rest if you want to feel the strength.**

*)**Rest your body and brain when needed. Not feeling the exhaustion does not mean everything is fine.**

*)**Do not be too hard on yourself whenever your memory is failing. Sometimes, the cause of the problem is you and not your brain.**

Making Brain Exercising a Habit

"An education isn't how much you have committed to memory, or even how much you know. It's being able to differentiate between what you know and what you don't."

- Anatole France

The brain needs exercising the same way the body does. This is the principle behind self-directed neuroplasticity; the new and most widely accepted theory behind the brain's full potential. As opposed to the old notion that the brain stays the same as far as nervous impulses and synapses "wiring" go, this newer theory highlights the importance of brain exercises to enhance it according to your needs and desires. Self-directed plasticity is now widely used in the treatment of brain injuries.

To start your mental workout, here is a list of the most effective brain exercises you can try without sacrificing the fun.

1. Crossword puzzles

Elders who regularly solve crossword puzzles have stronger retention and recalling ability. They also have 10 points more on their IQ and are more mentally cohesive than the average senior citizen. This has been the observation in a study involving Californians.

Particularly, crossword puzzle improves the linguistic and lexical intelligence of a person. This is a good start if you often fumble for words or just need to joggle you memory regularly.

2. Computation

Many people don't do this very basic brain exercise anymore. When was the last time you did a long computation manually, such as your grocery expense or utility bills? Although you can always go the convenient way using a calculator and an excel sheet, there is no need to totally shy away from mental arithmetic because the benefits are huge.

Make it a habit to do simple computations manually. If you are not confident with your answers, you can always double check with a calculator anyway. The important thing is that you practice your mathematical acumen and counting skills. Besides, don't you find it fulfilling to know you nailed a computation only using your hands and mind?

3. Video games

This may not be a traditional brain exercise, but playing video games is still an effective one. Contrary to popular belief, playing video games enhances brain activity by 50% because you are forced to push your mental agility to your highest. Your responses are more acute, and your brain-eye-hand coordination becomes more accurate.

As you play, your brain programs the different moves and strategies, so you can respond better and faster next time. That is already an application of neuroplasticity. This makes memorization and recalling faster for you.

Likewise, studies shows that children who play video games, when matched with proper learning habits, tend to score higher on IQ tests.

4. Sudoku

Even though Sudoku involves numbers and grids, it is actually more of a game of logic than math. The computation involved here is minimal, but the real test is really in the analytical part of the game. It trains your brain to look at a bigger picture and take into consideration every angle. By doing so, you are enhancing your analytical and visualization skills.

5. Journaling

Normally, a forgetful person has all the information stored in his brain. The recalling part makes the memory faulty. Usually, it is the person's inability to arrange data in his head according to a certain pattern, such as chronological order, association, or trigger, is the one causing forgetfulness.

To solve this, you have to practice juggling your memory on a daily basis, and that is by journaling your day. This brain exercise makes recalling a routine, which will mold your brain like how muscles grow with daily workouts. It also develops your vocabulary and mental cohesion, which you will definitely use in your profession.

6. Jigsaw puzzle

First marketed as a brain training aid because of its effectiveness in enhancing memory and increasing IQ, jigsaw puzzles are now one of the most popular hobbies of all time. The National Institutes of Health (NIH) acknowledges its effectiveness in improving visualization and analytical skills. At the same time, it tests your patience and concentration for the better; you are actually exercising your brain while having fun.

Key Points/Action Steps:

*)The brain needs exercising the same way your body does.

*)Make brain exercises a habit for bigger benefits.

*)To achieve the optimum neuroplasticity of your brain, you have to train it religiously like how you train your muscles repeatedly.

Enhancing Your Memory at Home

"Never make your home in a place. Make a home for yourself inside your own head. You'll find what you need to furnish it - memory, friends you can trust, love of learning, and other such things. That way it will go with you wherever you journey."

- Tad Williams

The home can be your own training center and learning institution. There are many ways to improve your memory and a lot of tools for you to enjoy and help you at the same time right in the comforts of your own home. Staying at home is no excuse to take your mental health for granted. Here are ways to enhance your memory at home.

1. Meditation

Where else is the best place to practice meditation but in the comfort of your home. This relaxation technique can enhance your brain's performance by 20%, with special improvement in your mental accuracy, clarity, and concentration. It also lowers your stress level by reducing cortisol and CRH (corticotropin-releasing hormone) – two hormones that speeds up the death of your brain neurons. Starting your day with meditation will also enhance the oxygen uptake to your brain whenever your exercise later on.

There are many meditation techniques to choose from, such as mindfulness technique and mind-body relaxation. All of them work. The important thing is that you make it a habit at least 15 minutes a day.

2. Intermittent fasting

Fasting is easier when at home because you have less temptation. Take advantage of it to unleash a sharper and more accurate memory.

Neuroscientist and author Dr. Michael Eades says intermittent fasting for 25 consecutive days, 16 straight hours a day, stimulates your brain's excretion of BDNF (Brain-Derived Neurotrophic Factor). It is a type of protein that ensures the consistency of nervous impulses by generating synapses as they die or get damaged. Synapses are your brain's "highway of information" which when left broken will also result in disruption of memory (this is where recalling becomes almost impossible). Aside from this effect, you will also get less distressed because of lower cortisol production.

Fasting for almost a month might be too intimidating to you. It is a good thing you have an alternative. According to Dr. Mark Mattson, another expert in neuroscience, people can do intermittent fasting; they just need to make sure that there are at least two days in between fasts. This is recommended for those who do not have bad memory to begin with but only want to improve it the fastest way possible.

Whatever you choose, both experts agree, you should be able to see the big difference just after a month from your last fasting.

3. Lumosity

The only reason why the game Lumosity is in this chapter is because it aims to change your gaming habits. Lumosity is a popular online gaming series specifically developed to increase IQ and memory. Developed using the neuroplasticity principles by the University of California at Berkeley, Stanford University, and University of Michigan, this series promises a more powerful brain just by playing it for 15 minutes a day. It is no hype as scientists certify its effectiveness, not to mention the 14 million users playing it on a regular basis.

It works on the five aspects of your brain all at the same time. Through its indexing system, you can monitor your progress by checking its Brain Performance Index (BPI). Just a warning though: this is addicting like any other online games, only it is truly worthwhile.

4. Put a pattern on your household chores

Acclimating yourself to mental patterns is better started at home where you have total control without the pressure of meeting a certain standard. Start by putting a pattern in your daily household chores, like the order of doing things, step-by-step routines, the time of task, etc. By doing so, you are putting organization back to your system, and your brain should be able to adopt it.

Usually, memory starts to lose its accuracy when the bits of information added with confused emotions become out of order. In such case, you are practically forgetting mental organization, so you just have to relearn and practice it.

5. Load your fridge with dark chocolates

Forget chips and burgers, dark chocolates are everything you need for snacks. Not only is dark chocolate good for your palate, it is also good for your memory.

First, dark chocolates are rich in antioxidants that will help protect your brain from oxidative stress and other damages caused by free radicals. A pure bar even contains more antioxidant than green tea and blueberry – not even close!

Second, dark chocolates have the right amount of caffeine to stimulate the brain – not too much like what is in your coffee (decaffeinated included). It is a good snack for students reviewing lessons at home or for professionals who have to take their work home.

Lastly, dark chocolates have a high concentration of phenylethylamine, a type of feel-good hormone that gives the feeling of being in love. It also increases the production of endorphin to fight mental and emotional stress, as well as, serve as your natural pain reliever.

6. Perform breathing exercise

Breathing exercise is more than a relaxation technique. It also helps your memory improve in three ways.

First, slow and deep breathing induces relaxation that can help you think clearer and faster. It also calms your senses, so you can focus only on memorization or recalling.

Second, deliberate deep breathing increases the absorption rate of oxygen for your brain. Optimum oxygen uptake means bigger brain for you, literally.

Lastly, scientists found out regularly practicing breathing exercise specifically enhances the function of the hippocampus, the region of your brain in charge of recalling and sending electrical impulses called Theta wave.

Key Points/Action Steps:

*)Improving your memory is very much possible even while staying at home.

*)Stressful household chores can become memory enhancers if you will look at them in a different way.

*)Improving your memory is possible even while resting or having fun.

Sharpen Your Memory with Physical Activities

"Thinking is like exercise, it requires consistency and rigor. Like barbells in a weightlifting room, the classics force us to either put them down or exert our minds. They require us to think."

- Oliver DeMille

Studies show physical activities in general can enhance the brain's performance especially in the memorization department. The mind-body connection is so overpowering that not having the two in synch will cause either one to fall apart.

Initially, experts believed exercising is important to preserve sharp memory to improve blood circulation, which in effect increases the supply of oxygen to the brain. However, further studies discovered the connection is deeper than first assumed.

Here is a deeper look at physical activities and their importance in sharpening your memory. Try these exercises to keep your body fit and your memory sharp.

1. Jogging

Do not underestimate this simple yet effective cardio exercise because doing it for only 20 minutes is enough to increase the brain's size; thus, also increasing its performance. Researchers from the University of California at Irvine discovered this when they were trying to figure out how mere cardio exercises provided significant boost in memory tests. To achieve the best results, jog before your day starts.

2. Yoga

Harvard-based psychiatrist Dr. John Ratey recommends performing yoga for 10 minutes every day because it is a great way to incorporate relaxation with physical activity without straining the body like when you do heavy workouts. According to him, it significantly enhances blood circulation that in effect increases the oxygen supply to the brain. At the same time, it induces relaxation and mental clarity because of the meditation that naturally comes with the practice.

You can try yoga nidra (lucid dreaming) and bhramari pranayam (physical and breathing yoga matched with meditation).

3. Stretching

Not everyone considers stretching an actual physical activity. However, this is more than enough to improve your memory for two reasons. First, stretching for 10 to 15 minutes early in the day sets your body's phase and enhances blood flow to the brain. More oxygen means healthier brain, right? Second, stretching stimulates your body's excretion of feel-good hormones that will allow your brain to work faster and harder. Studies have confirmed a person who feels happy and relaxed memorizes and recalls better than someone who is emotionally unstable.

4. Stationary biking

In a Swiss study, experts discovered stationary biking at least 40 minutes three times a week could significantly reduce your cortisol level while increasing your brain's oxygen uptake, as compared to other cardio exercises also improves blood circulation. What makes this exercise better is the fact it does not strain the body as a whole and only focuses on the respiration (remember hat heavy workout increases cortisol).

Key Points/Action Steps:

*)The body needs proper exercises in order to benefit the brain.

*)Seasonal exercising won't do; you have to do it regularly, preferably on a daily basis.

*)Heavy workouts, such as strength and resistance training, that are good for the muscles are not always the best for the brain.

Taking Memory-Enhancing Herbal Remedies

"Just as food eaten without appetite is a tedious nourishment, so does study without zeal damage the memory by not assimilating what it absorbs."

- Leonardo da Vinci

Eastern medicine has not always been in the same playing field as Western medicine, the latter receiving the more attention and interest in the past. However, as alternative medicine becomes more accepted, they need further scientific studies to back up their claims. Now, even medical doctors agree memory enhancement is possible with certain herbal remedies.

Here is the list.

1. *Bacopa monnieri*

Also known as brahmi, this plant has already been scrutinized in a research published in the *Journal of Alternative and Complementary Medicine.* Experts say it delays dementia and Alzheimer's disease while sharpening the memory, giving even old people the ability to recall just as if they were still young. They suggest drinking brewed dried leaves gives the same benefit of a 300-milligram capsule, its supplement counterpart.

Furthermore, it also shows promise in managing ADHD, allergy, anxiety disorders, and irritable bowel syndrome (IBS) in younger people.

2. Green tea

You need this for three reasons. First, it is very high in antioxidants that can fight free radicals that can damage your brain. Second, it can prevent inflammation, which is also a common reason of temporary memory decline. Third, it contains a phytochemical called EGCG (epigallocatechin galate), a chemical that is proven to induce neurogenesis, the natural formation of new neurons in your brain that is necessary to maintain "youthful" performance and processing of stored information.

3. Rosemary

Two significant studies prove that it is more than a spice in your kitchen or scent in your bathroom.

In the journal *Therapeutic Advances in Psychopharmacology*, it was observed that a significant boost in cognitive ability alongside the natural preservation of memory. It makes memorization more accurate and faster.

Second, a published study in the *International Journal of Neuroscience* found that the rosmarinic acid and carnosic acid of this plant are potent enough to protect the brain cells from natural damages brought by aging.

4. Panax ginseng

Contrary to marketing claims, panax ginseng does not significantly boost memory by enhancing recalling ability. However, it greatly helps in the process of memorization because it improves mental concentration and accuracy, perfect for students and professionals who need to memorize a lot of details all the time.

5. Huperzine

It is not as famous as the other ones on this list, but initial studies suggest it can be the next big thing when it comes to memory enhancement the Ayurvedic way. It captures interest in the medical field simply because huperzine can somehow replicate the effects of real drugs for Alzheimer's disease.

You are probably wondering why the most famous memory-enhancing herb – gingko biloba – is not on the list. Sorry to disappoint you but that herb is nothing more than a product of shrewd marketing hype. The *Journal of the American Medical Association* reported in 2009 that although gingko biloba showed promise in protecting the hippocampus in the brain, there was no solid link between this benefit and memory enhancement – only normal nutritional value that makes it like any nutritious herbal plant.

Key Points/Action Steps:

*)Try to integrate herbal medicine with your dose of conventional memory-boosting routines for better results.

*)Replace your regular cup of coffee with these healthy and brain-friendly herbal remedies.

*)Always consult your doctor if you are taking medications to prevent adverse reactions.

Eating Memory-Boosting Foods

"Feasting is also closely related to memory. We eat certain things in a particular way in order to remember who we are. Why else would you eat grits in Madison, New Jersey?"

- *Jeff Smith*

What's good for the body is good for the brain. That is true. However, what is good for the brain is not always the best for your memory. Feeding your brain with the right nutrition does not always equate to optimum memory because some foods are meant to work better with the other aspects of your health. For instance, fiber-rich foods are best for your digestion while those containing high ascorbic acid work best for your immune system. If you specifically need memory enhancement, eating random healthy foods might not suffice.

You can fill your plate with the best memory-boosting foods, and you can start with the foods on this list.

1. Blueberries

Adding a cup of blueberries to your diet everyday prevents oxidative stress which can lead to accelerated age-related memory degeneration caused by dementia or Alzheimer's. Dr. Steven Pratt of California's Scripps Memorial Hospital added that it does not only save your precious memory but also enhances your learning capabilities, particularly motor skills.

2. Avocado

Many people avoid it because it contains the highest fat content among all fruits. Nonetheless, surprisingly, its monounsaturated fats actually help lower blood cholesterol and blood pressure. What's more is that it enhanced blood flow to the brain, which keeps it more active and well-supplied with oxygen. Dr. Pratt recommends eating half of it a day.

3. Wild Salmon

Being a deep-water fish makes it clean, but the best part of it is its high omega-3 fatty acid content. Numerous studies have already confirmed that omega-3 enhances oxygen uptake to the brain while lowering inflammation that can result to long-term damage. Regularly eating foods high in omega-3, wild salmon in particular, also delays the onset of Alzheimer's disease and dementia, in case you are historically prone to them.

4. Seeds and nuts

Seeds, such as sunflower seeds and flax seeds, and nuts, such as walnuts, chestnuts, hazelnuts, cashews, and almonds, are all high in vitamin E that has been proven to prevent cognitive decline as you age. Choosing them as your snack will also make you think and understand faster. Eat an ounce a day to get the best benefits.

5. Whole grains

Eating oatmeal, brown rice, or whole-grain breads every morning does more than improve your digestion and lower your cholesterol. According to Dr. Ann Kulze, a well-known author and diet specialist, whole grains are some of the best memory-booster because they have everything your brain needs – fiber, vitamin E, and omega-3. Of course, a healthy heart also gives you a healthy brain.

Key Points/Action Steps:

*)Choose foods for your brain and heart, not for your tongue alone.

*)Make these foods a staple of your grocery list.

*)Cook and serve them in variety to maintain your appetite.

Adding Memory-Enhancing Supplements to Your Diet

"Seek out the memories depression takes away and project them into the future. Be brave; be strong; take your pills."

- Andrew Solomon

As the term implies, dietary supplements are not meant to take over the role of real foods. They are only here to give your brain an extra boost, especially if you cannot maintain a variety of appropriate diet. Nonetheless, choosing the best ones for your brain will help you preserve your memory for a long time, even when you are already past your prime. Starting young reaps better results, so you might want to change your supplementation now.

Here are memory-enhancing supplements that should definitely be in your medicine cabinet.

1. Vitamin E

Vitamin E stops age-related memory decline by protecting the brain cells from oxidative stress. This way, the lifespan of your brain cells are extended even if they should naturally die faster when you are past your prime. A study also concludes it can delay the development of certain mental disorders, such as dementia and Alzheimer's disease.

2. Vitamin B12

As aforementioned in a previous chapter, vitamin B12 deficiency is one of the most common culprits of memory decline. However, you will need more than your daily recommended 6mcg allowance (RDA) to make the most out of it. Take B-vitamin complex that contains at least 15mcg, or equivalent to the 250% of your RDA.

3. Omega-3 fatty acid

Not everyone has the privilege to spend for salmons, tuna, fresh sardines, and mackerel everyday. Thus, taking 1000mg of omega-3 fatty acid with at least 180% DHA is necessary. Researchers in New Zealand's Massey University believe it is the new wonder supplement for the brain. It lowers risk of inflammation in the brain, boosts blood flow and oxygen uptake to the brain, and delays the progression of Alzheimer's and dementia – what else can you ask for.

Here is a bonus benefit for you: It is also said to boost libido on both sexes and the erection in men.

4. CoQ10

CoQ10 or CoEnzyme Q10 also works like omega-3 by improving blood flow to the brain and protecting the cells from free radicals. It is best for the heart that in a way benefits the brain. There are also claims it can fight mental disorders, although no concrete study has yet to prove that.

5. Acetyl-L-carnitine

It shows promise in reversing the effects of Alzheimer's disease to one's memory, but the biggest news here is its capacity to slow down memory decline brought by mental disorders. As an amino acid, it works best for your muscles and metabolism. However, the general interest from the scientific community is enough to make it one of the priority supplements you have to take.

Key Points/Action Steps

*)Make dietary supplementation a regular part of our diet.

*)Choose supplements that best address your memory concerns, such as the ones listed here.

*)Never make these supplements, or any supplement for that matter, a replacement to real food.

How to Apply What You've Learned?

This book will not be able to help you if you refuse to accept what has been shared with you. Thus, you have to religiously follow the steps and embrace a new lifestyle for good.

Remember the key ideas from this ebook:

*)**Memory decline is not permanent. You do not have to worry too much because that will just make matters worse.**

*)**There are quick fixes to do when your memory is failing you.**

*)**Make brain exercising a habit continuously developing your mental power.**

*)**Adapt a healthy lifestyle that is good for the body and brain.**

*)**The home can be your own training center and learning facility. Do not stop learning new things and honing your memory even while at home.**

*)**The brain is like a muscle; it needs exercising to grow.**

*)**Support your mental and physical health with the right herbal drinks, foods, and supplements.**

How To Boost Your Creativity

In today's modern creative economy, one of the most critical skills to possess is being creative. People who are creative are marked by their dedication to their craft, their patience, their ability to think outside of the proverbial box, and their willingness to take risks. These traits are essential not only in completing artistic pursuits, but also in forging greater happiness in your life. The succeeding chapters discuss in greater detail why creativity is important and what you can do to become a creative person yourself.

Lending Appreciation to the Value of Creativity

"Others have seen what is and asked why. I have seen what could be and asked why not."

– Pablo Picasso

If there is a glaring pitfall in the current pedagogical system used in educational institutions across the country today, it is the fact that it leaves very little room for students to develop creativity. Most of the time, students are subjected to rigid school policies that prevent them from veering from the established curriculum or else face stiff penalties from school administrators.

Instead, students are taught to toe the line and finish their studies so they can automatically be aligned to a predefined future. This future, more often than not, involves being a lifelong employee to giant corporations, building a domestic life, growing old at a retirement community, and finally passing away. Nowhere can the emphasis on creativity be found in this preset timetable.

The lack of focus on fostering individual creativity can pose problems in the long run, especially in light of the emerging creative economy. Where once the focus used to be on manual labor before it gradually shifted to industrialized operations, these days success can be had by those who can present the most creative solutions to modern industry problems, including design, e-commerce, engineering, communication, and finance. In other words, at no other time is the ability to think outside of the box more pressing than at the current period.

A life of creativity

But being creative and exercising it in your day to day life need not be grand or life-changing. In fact, creativity is something that can be applied even in the most mundane or quotidian of situations. For instance, whiling away time at a cafe waiting for your friend to arrive can be spent writing or sketching. At the subway, being observant and mindful of your fellow passengers can yield the much-needed inspiration you need for your next creative project.

The key is to develop the tools needed to exercise creativity as part of your lifestyle. While some people may seem naturally inclined to be creative in their endeavors, take heart in the fact that creativity is a skill that can be learned over time.

The succeeding chapters highlight the traits that mark a creative individual and what you can do to kick start a life of utter creativity.

Today's creative economy calls for greater individual creativity.

Identifying the Traits of a Creative Individual

"Creativity is a habit, and the best creativity is the result of good work habits."

– Twyla Tharp

Many people are discouraged from exercising creativity in their day to day lives simply because they refuse to acknowledge their capacity to be creative themselves. Often, you will hear them say, "But I'm not an artist," or "I don't have it in me to be creative," as if one is born either with or without creative genes.

But the fact is, the biological component of creativity is one that is still subject to greater tests and studies. In the meantime, creativity should not be treated as a genetic trait, but rather as a skill that you can acquire through education and practice. In other words, with discipline and an ample amount of will, anyone can be a creative individual.

There are a number of traits that distinguish a creative person. These are the same traits that shape and define their capacity for greater imagination, which they use either in their everyday tasks, their work, or in their spare time. Some of these traits include the following:

Creative people are naturally curious.

If you want to develop your creativity skills, you would need to be mindful of everything around you because each little thing corresponds to a certain meaning or symbol. Being curious means you do not merely take interest in something, you also take concrete actions to turn this thing into something novel.

Part of this trait is the ability to ask questions: what does this thing stand for? How is it meaningful? What can I use it for?

Creative people are willing to try out new experiences.

You shouldn't be limited by your existing knowledge and experience. Creativity calls for constant growth and development. Learning and relearning things is an integral part of unleashing your potential to create. If you are into visual arts, for example, you should be well-versed with different styles, brush strokes, and painting techniques. It is only by studying these different facets of painting will you discover your own unique style.

Creative people are patient.

While it is generally understood that creative people have a lot of ideas running in their heads, they are also the first to acknowledge that they can only do one thing at a time. The only way to finish a project is by sporting patience and commitment to it. Otherwise, you end up with piles of unfinished works that do not at all convey what you wish to express. For writers, this means enduring the often laborious process of researching, writing a draft, editing, and proofreading before finishing a written output. Despite the volume of work involved, it's best to consider the finished output as the reward to all your labor.

Creative people are goal-oriented.

Sure, you may have a sudden burst of creativity, enough for you to sing, dance, paint, or write. But despite their sporadic nature, these little acts of creative expression form a part of the bigger picture, which includes your goals of becoming better at what you are doing. Each thing you do reinforces these goals. So if you find yourself sketching a portrait, for example, you know this is part of your bigger goal of becoming a better visual artist.

Creative people think outside of the box.

This is what separates ordinary thinkers from creative thinkers; the latter do not confine themselves within strict and dogmatic restrictions. They are compelled to see things from a different angle, not for the sake of being different, but to underscore the fact that there is more than one way of looking at things. Mastering this skill is indubitably a hallmark of creative people.

Creative people are willing to take risks and are unafraid to fail.

Fear of failure and of the unknown is one of the reasons that hampers the creative growth of many people. If you aspire to be more creative, you should be able to overcome this debilitating fear. The succeeding chapters will discuss in greater detail some strategies that you can subscribe to in order to be more fearless and daring as you develop your creative skills.

Creativity is a skill that can be learned over time. Some of the traits creative people share include being naturally curious, sporting intense dedication to their craft, and having the ability to think outside of the box.

Identifying the Challenges that Hamper Creative Growth

"Great minds discuss ideas. Average minds discuss events. Small minds discuss people."

– Eleanor Roosevelt

Before proceeding to the discussion of what you can do to boost your creativity, it is important to first identify some of the most common challenges that hamper your creativity. The point is to understand where these problems are coming from and what you can do to eventually overcome them.

The chief obstacle to creativity are self-doubts and insecurities. Being creative calls for confidence and a semblance of self-assurance. If you are perennially on your toes because of imagined monsters, it would be very difficult to sport an openness to ideas—something that is doubtlessly crucial in the creative process.

Most insecurities come from unresolved issues in the past. Take a step back and try to figure out the root of your fears. Did you grow up in an environment where you were constantly called out for every little infraction you've committed? Were you subjected to intense pressure growing up? Were you bullied by your peers? Did you grow up thinking you don't have anyone whom you can fully trust?

These sort of issues obviously take time to heal. Often, however, the first step in coming to terms with your past is in acknowledging it. There's no point in trying to forget things in your past as if they did not happen. They did. The more you deny them, the more these ghosts will haunt you.

Doing away with self-hate

Another factor that hampers creativity is excessive self-criticism. It is totally fine to be self-critical, but not to the point where you fail to find anything satisfying in yourself. Excessive self-criticism is almost paramount to self-hate. And if there's anything you should do, it is to learn how to love yourself. The sooner you learn to accept your limitations and weaknesses, the easier it becomes for you to take steps to better yourself.

Complacency is when you are not doing anything to improve your knowledge or your circumstances in general. You are so used to the current set-up, so much so that you avoid changing anything in your life. As far as creativity is concerned, this can be a bad thing, especially since being creative requires a certain degree of dynamism.

But the greatest obstacle, perhaps, to fostering creativity in your life is the fear of failure. When you are afraid of committing mistakes, you provide yourself very minimal chance to grow and learn. This fear will be discussed in greater depth in the next chapters.

In order to foster greater creativity in your life, you need to overcome the challenges that hamper your creative growth. Some of these challenges include insecurities, excessive self-criticism, tendency to be complacent, and fear of failure.

Creating a Sense of Self-Awareness

"Passion is one great force that unleashes creativity, because if you're passionate about something, then you're more willing to take risks."

- Yo-Yo Ma

It's not enough that you are creative merely for the sake of being creative. Far more important is your ability to channel your creativity in creating something tangible and real. Without the actual creation process, your creative skills will remain in your head and will not therefore be fully consummated.

On this end, it is necessary for you to sport a sense of self-awareness in order to identify the things that you are passionate about or deeply interested in. Knowing what your passions are will allow you to put your creativity to good use because then your actions will be dictated by clear and specific goals. This way, you do away with random activities that do not serve any real purpose over the long term.

For some people, for example, photography counts as one of their passions. Most ordinary camera owners would just point and shoot with little regard for such technicalities as aperture, shutter speed, or the rule of thirds.

Deliberate, not accidental

But creativity calls for something more than the usual. If you are serious about photography, it is incumbent upon you to exercise greater creativity with each shot you take. In this sense, your photos become deliberate outputs of your creativity, with due attention to the technical details that other people wouldn't normally pay attention to. Your photos are not merely accidental, and this is precisely what lends them greater depth.

This sense of self-awareness should not just apply to your strengths. You should also have a clear idea of what your perceived weaknesses are. This will allow you to work on them in the hopes of turning them into strengths, or at the very least will instruct you about the limits of what you can do.

On the same note, get rid of distractions. More than anyone else, you should have an idea of what your potential distractions are. Do you get easily distracted by email or SMS notifications on your phone? Then turn it off or put it on silent mode while you are engaging in a creative exercise. Do you get distracted by cable news channels? Then turn off the TV, or better yet, get it out of your room.

In sum, the more self-aware you are, the more manageable it becomes for you to channel your creativity into things that you are passionate about.

Creating a sense of self-awareness is critical in the exercise of your creative skills.

Living Outside of Your Bubble

"For me, insanity is super sanity. The normal is psychotic. Normal means lack of imagination, lack of creativity."

— Jean Dubuffet

If your goal is to foster creativity as a natural part of your life, it is necessary that you immerse yourself in an environment where such a goal can be met and realized. Creativity demands a dynamic environment where you are constantly engaged by the things that you see, hear, and feel. Without such dynamism, it would be very difficult, if not altogether impossible, to unleash your potential to be creative.

A good writer, for example, isn't content with just sitting behind a desk all day, typing away words as if devoid of context. It is often said that the best writers are those who try to experience things, those who are unafraid to get out of their comfort zones, all in the name of living life before eventually distilling it into words. All told, there is wisdom and greater depth in writing about things you have actually felt and experienced as opposed to things that you have merely conjured up in your head.

The same principle applies in other creative pursuits. If you want to have a wider perspective of things and gain a wealth of experience to draw inspiration from, it is necessary that you get yourself out there and take in as much insight as you can. How? Here are a number of ways to get you started with learning how to get out of your comfort zone:

Don't stop learning.

Read as many books as you can, watch as much stuff as you can, and listen to as much music as you can. Allot time to do any of these things to keep your mind from going stagnant.

You want your imagination to work on overdrive, not remain static. The worst thing that can happen to you is when your head goes blank when asked to come up with something.

Many artists and intellectuals are consummate learners. These people are keenly aware of the fact that in order for them to be better at what they do, they need to keep themselves abreast of the news and trends both within and beyond their respective fields. This is precisely the reason why things such as continuing education and professional skills trainings are still offered. It is to ensure that you make improvements on, rather than completely unlearn, your skills.

Get on the road.

Exploring places and appreciating cultures different from yours constitutes an enriching way to learn and experience new things. Traveling is often said to be a self-rewarding exercise in that you pick up valuable lessons along the way. These lessons can either be realizations about yourself and the things you see around or the people you interact with.

When traveling, make it a point to be particularly observant. If possible, bring along a small notebook and a pen so that you can write down your thoughts while on the road. Be especially mindful of the scents you smell, the culinary fare you get to try out, the destinations you see, and the nuances of the culture you immerse yourself in. Try to make the whole thing a sensory experience. Inspiration will come sooner or later.

Meet new people.

While it is true that spending some alone time induces creativity, the same is true when you are in the company of other people. So instead of shying away from social situations, treat these as learning opportunities.

See, part of nurturing creativity is the ability to share knowledge and possibly collaborate with others. Learn from the people you interact with and impart insights to others, too. You will realize that fresh perspectives or ideas different from yours work wonders in defining your own perspective of things.

The fact is, the collaborative aspect of creativity is integral not only in the completion of big-scale projects, such as filming a full-length feature or designing a building, but is more particularly integral in the actual learning process. This is best exemplified by children working together on an arts and craft project, which teaches them the values of mutual respect and team work on top of the usual need to exercise creativity.

Creativity is fostered by engaging yourself in new insights and experiences beyond your comfort zone.

Understanding the Perils of Perfectionism

"Have no fear of perfection, you'll never reach it."

– Salvador Dali

Nothing is more attractive than the idea of perfection. It's certainly a beautiful thing to consider, especially when it comes to the fulfillment of your creative ideas. Of course, you want these ideas to turn out perfectly, so much so that achieving something short of perfect is not good enough.

Part of our fascination with perfection lies in its inherent impossibility. At the same time, it also has something to do with our own imperfect nature, where striving for perfection ultimately becomes a way of transcending our own imperfections.

However, is there such a thing as perfection? Conventional wisdom tells us there isn't, and the closest you could get to achieving it lies in giving your all in every pursuit you choose to undertake.

As such, the idea of perfection is a myth. The concept itself is not only unattainable; it is unsustainable, too. For instance, after having achieved perfection, what else would there be to strive for? Perfection signifies the zenith of success from which there is no other way to go but down. If you are striving to foster a culture of creativity in your life, you would want a constant state of growth and development, not to get stuck in a place where you are left to do nothing while basking in a delusional sense of triumph.

Given its unattainability, to subscribe to the notion of perfection, therefore, is to set yourself up for failure and disappointment. The more you strive for it, the more you realize how impossible it is to achieve it. The more disillusioned you are, the harder it becomes to motivate yourself to keep going and to keep your creative juice flowing.

Here are other reasons why perfectionism is not an ideal mindset to sport insofar as developing your creativity is concerned:

Perfectionism creates completely unnecessary tension and stress. When everything you or others do is not always up to your unreasonable standards, you are in effect raising the stress level not only for yourself but for others, too. When will these standards be met? Probably never, so there's that.

Perfectionism stifles your creative growth. You want nothing less than perfect, so obviously you leave little room for spontaneity, which is a key element of being creative. You tend to be overly cautious of everything you are doing, even to the point of micromanaging the most insignificant details. In this sense, cautiousness becomes your guiding principle—something that isn't really helpful at all in promoting greater creativity.

Aiming for perfection can be very self-limiting. When you refuse to entertain things that you think will not lead to perfection, you are essentially shutting off opportunities that may help you in the future.

Being a perfectionist takes away the fun in what you do and eventually breeds unhappiness. Being creative should be fun, engaging, and mentally stimulating, not scary and terrorizing. When the fear of failure and coming up short of your personal expectations becomes the rule in your life, dissatisfaction and guilt come about as the likely results. Where's the fun in that?

In sum, your sense of creativity should not be stifled by a misplaced sense of perfection. At the very least, your goals and expectations should be tempered by an ample dose of realism and reasonableness. There is nothing wrong in exacting high standards to yourself and your capabilities, unless these standards become the very same reason that brings you unhappiness, self-doubt, and the inability to grow.

Striving for perfection in your creative pursuits limits your growth and sets you up for disappointment. The best way to foster creativity is by allowing yourself to grow through your mistakes and by giving your best shot in everything you do.

Aiming for Sustainability

"You can't use up creativity. The more you use, the more you have."

– Maya Angelou

The thing about creativity is that it needs to be sustainable. This means that it should become an integral part of your life over the long term and not just over a brief period of time. The more deeply rooted creativity is in your life, the greater its impact becomes.

So how do you exactly make creativity an integral part of your day to day life? Here are a few important pointers to remember:

Embrace creativity as part of your life.

From the clothes you choose to wear to the way you design your apartment, almost all aspects of your life entails varying degrees of creativity. As such, there is actually very little excuse to not exercise your creative skills. But instead of treating these instances as chores you need to get done and over with, a better approach would be to take them as valuable learning opportunities.

Allot part of your schedule for some alone time.

Many experts argue that you are at your most creative when you are alone. When there are no other people around to disrupt your thoughts, you become in touch with your ideas and concepts. Make it a point to allocate time, even for only an hour, each day for you to be alone with yourself. This is a great way to foster discipline and to render a sense of regularity to your creativity sessions.

Learn the value of collaboration.

Even if you spend some time to be alone with your thoughts, do not completely disregard the value of collaboration. Being with other like-minded individuals is a great way to stimulate creativity and lend more fun to the actual activities. Remember that exercising creativity need not be very academic, and practicing it with other people guarantees that it will become a dynamic and an engaging experience.

Keep a journal.

If you want to keep track of your progress, keeping a journal is definitely the way to go. Writing down your thoughts, ideas, insights, and the actions you've taken to concretize your ideas allows you to assess how much you have learned and how much more effort you need to give to be better.

Indeed, creativity is something that you should learn to integrate in your day to day activities. It is only by doing so will it become deeply entrenched in your psyche.

Embracing creativity as part of your life is crucial in ensuring its sustainability.

Promoting a Healthy Body for a Healthy Mind

"There is no time for cut-and-dried monotony. There is time for work. And time for love. That leaves no other time."

– Coco Chanel

You have probably come across the idea of the starving artist—a broke, physically frail, and emotionally tortured soul yearning for nothing more than to create art that will encapsulate his or her inner struggles. Although largely bleak, this image romanticizes poverty and hunger as if these two concepts were requisites in inspiring creativity.

But now is as good a time as any to debunk this notion. For the fact is, fostering creativity does not only require a healthy sense of imagination. More importantly, it demands a sound physical state, which is essential if you want to optimize your potentials.

Consider this: how will it be possible to sustain your creativity if you are in a bad physical form? Even at schools, the emphasis on having healthy bodies through healthy lifestyle choices is underscored to all students. It should be no different for adults.

At the end of the day, you are able to think well and be on the top of your game if you are in great physical shape. You end up having more energy to do things, think clearly, and take concrete measures designed to bring your ideas into reality.

Kick starting a healthy lifestyle

Thankfully, there are a lot of things that you can do to kick start a healthy lifestyle, beginning of course with the quality of your dietary intake. The key lies in moderation. Avoid overeating, or conversely, eating too little. Watch out for the kind of food you consume. Make sure you don't end up eating food items that contain excessive amounts of cholesterol, sodium, MSG, and salt. Strive to achieve the required daily calorie intake for adults.

Closely related to having balanced meals is the need to do away with unhealthy habits, such as smoking and binge drinking. Smoking is a highly addictive activity that poses serious risks to your overall health condition. The same is true with drinking too much, which increases your chances of acquiring a number of gastro-intestinal disorders.

Complement your healthy dietary intake with a physically active lifestyle. The less sedentary you are, the better. As such, allot part of your schedule for regular workouts and adhere to it. Remember that you should be disciplined and committed enough to stick to your regular workouts.

You can work out either at the comfort of your own home or at a gym. At home, you get a greater sense of comfort and ease because you are already familiar with the environment. At the same time, you can multitask and do other tasks while working out. Just make sure to do proper research on the exercises you intend to carry out to make sure they match your immediate needs.

On the other hand, working out at the gym provides you access to pieces of equipment and tools to help you achieve your fitness goals. A certified fitness instructor is also on hand to assist you in coming up with a personalized workout routine designed to address your physical needs.

Confidence-booster

The importance of working out couldn't be emphasized enough. While having regular workouts boosts your stamina and improves your body's defenses against infections and diseases, its benefits are not merely limited to your overall physical condition. In fact, numerous studies point out that having a healthy body allows you to feel better about yourself, and is therefore instrumental in the development of self-confidence and a more solid sense of self-worth.

Aside from working out, do take time to engage in sports and outdoor recreational activities too. Taking part in sports not only enhances your physical form and sharpens your mental focus, it also fosters discipline and sportsmanship—valuable lessons that you can certainly apply in your quest to be more creative in your life.

Similarly, devoting part of your time for outdoor recreational activities can be a reinvigorating exercise. These activities provide for moments of introspection, which can be very useful in conjuring up ideas. Communing with nature is also a great way to draw much-needed inspiration.

Inspiring creativity requires not just a healthy mind, but also a healthy body.

Doing Away with the Fear of Failure

"Creativity is allowing yourself to make mistakes. Art is knowing which ones to keep."

– Scott Adams

Have you ever found yourself hesitating to embark on a project because you were afraid you would mess it up? Have you passed up on opportunities because you were convinced you weren't good enough for them? Have you given up on the notion that you are capable of great things?

If you answered in the affirmative to any of the questions above, then you may be harboring a debilitating fear of losing or failing.

In the course of inspiring greater creativity in your life, it is necessary, paramount even, to lose this sort of fear from your system. More than anything, this fear does nothing other than magnify the slim probability of failing, which should not really matter in the grand scheme of things. The more you entertain thoughts of failing, the tougher it gets for you to sport a positive outlook with regard to your capabilities.

Here are a few tricks to get over your fear of failing:

Don't pay too much attention to what others are saying or what you think they will say. Otherwise, you would be wasting your energy by dwelling on completely irrelevant things. Who cares what they think about you, right? Besides, these same folks are probably too busy with their own lives to bother themselves with your failures.

Improve your self-esteem. The fear of failure is often associated with an unhealthy sense of self. You probably think you are not skilled enough or that you are not smart enough to ever do anything significant. You're wrong. Practice positive reinforcement and believe that you have what it takes to succeed.

Sport a can-do attitude. If you think you can, then you can.

Stop looking at things around you as you would an exam. No one is out to castigate you in case you fail. Neither will there be anyone to call you out for missing the required mark. Loosen up and get rid of your inhibitions.

Start small and grow from there. Your fear of failure may be rooted in your unreasonable and unrealistic goals or expectations. If this is the case, learn to deal with small things first before branching out to bigger endeavors. If you have a hard time writing a novel, then maybe you can break it down to individual chapters first. This way you don't shock or scare yourself needlessly.

Learn to manage stress. When you are overpowered by stress, you lose the will to exercise creativity. Give yourself a break and take a breather if you must. Don't pressure yourself into doing something you have no way of completing. Gauge yourself and take action only once you feel you are ready.

Remember that your failures do not define you as a person. So learn to let go of your fear of failure in order to fully embrace a life of creativity.

The fear of failure can be very debilitating. In developing greater creativity, it is necessary to get rid of this fear.

Nurturing the Creative Spirit Over the Long Term

"Creativity is everything. It is the preview of life's coming attractions."

- Albert Einstein

As has been sufficiently underscored in the previous chapters, creativity is not a one-time exercise. To become deeply ingrained in your character, it has to be sustained over the long term. As such, it would do well for you to try to exercise your creative skills in everything you do.

Begin by dedicating a regular schedule for your creative pursuits. Doing so will help you get used to including creativity sessions in your daily itinerary. Regularity in exercising creativity is important because just as it is in any other field, such as sports, you need to put in time and effort to become better at what you are doing.

But regularity does not in any way imply predictability. Shake up your routine every now and then, particularly when you feel you are getting too comfortable with your routine. The key is to always find a reason to be excited.

Be in the company of creative people. Learn from them and be motivated with their work ethic, value to their skills, and capacity to exceed expectations. Take their experiences and successes as a springboard from which to launch your own creative pursuits.

Fun as motivation

Have fun, too. Being creative entails imagination and the ability to think outside of the box. Without the fun element, the entire process would seem bleak and too academic. Use fun as a motivation for you to keep going.

And finally, reward yourself. Although creativity by itself should serve as its own reward, it doesn't hurt to reinforce your commitment to be more creative by incentivizing your hard work and valuable time spent. In addition, this should not in any way be misconstrued as an act of vanity because it isn't. What this does is merely to motivate you to work harder and give your best shot every time.

So after finishing, say, an arts and craft project, treat yourself with life's little pleasures, such as a warm bath or a cup of cocoa. You can also allow yourself to take a break in order to relax and get yourself excited as you plan out your next project.

In sum, fostering greater creativity in your life is possible, particularly when you are disciplined and driven enough to succeed. When sustained over the long term, creativity can be very useful in defining your character and in turning your great ideas into reality.

So get yourself ready on this exciting journey to unleash your fullest potential. Now is as good a time as any to get started.

Boosting your creativity is not a one-time exercise. You should take measures to ensure your sense of creativity is nurtured over the long term.

How to Apply Key Ideas for the Best Results?

Although creativity is a skill that you can learn over time, know that it needs to be sustained and integrated into your day to day affairs so that it can really take root and become part of your life. Treat your failures as opportunities to learn and be better. Do not be afraid of them. At the same time, look at your successes as an affirmation of your discipline and commitment to your craft. Most importantly, treat creativity as a self-rewarding exercise. The more creative you become, the greater happiness you derive and the more meaningful your life becomes.

How To Find Your Talents And Strengths

"How to Find Your Talents: Simple Ideas for Finding Your Talents and Strengths" is a simple compendium that is written to help out individuals who have not found out their talents and gifts yet.

The tips presented here are very simple to follow and the simplicity of the suggestions will give you more motivation. You will not have any excuses not to follow the tips presented here.

This collection presents ten chapters reinforced with examples and key points.

Enjoy reading this book! Show the world your talent soon.

Know Yourself

"A human being has so many skins inside, covering the depths of the heart. We know so many things, but we don't know ourselves! Why, thirty or forty skins or hides, as thick and hard as an ox's or bear's, cover the soul. Go into your own ground and learn to know yourself there."

– Meister Eckhart

It is easy to find your true talent when you know who you are. By knowing what lies within, you will know ultimately what you want. This is the major requisite for achieving fulfillment and true happiness.

If the experiences you face and the things that you do are all aligned to the things that you truly want, there is a higher probability for you to attract elements into your life that will make you happy. Experts say that this is the key towards having a truly meaningful life. In essence, in order to find your talent, you have to work less and live more.

But are there activities that will actually help you in the process of knowing yourself better? Actually there are lots of them. Here are some activities highly recommended by experts:

Do some meditation

Regular meditation is the key towards quieting your mind. When you're successful in quieting your mind, you can enjoy inner peace, balance, and true joy. This is the major condition required for acquiring more knowledge. This way, you can be more open with less judgment involved.

Expose your core values

Observe how you react to situations and find the time to analyze what your core values are. Every once in a while, do some introspection or reflection to examine and analyze your own values. That way, you will not only find your true interests, you will find more reasons live the next days to the fullest. Instead of dwelling on other people's expectations, why not try to make a set of your own. When you finally figure out what you truly want to do, then you will be able to plan accordingly what you will do without deviating from the top values that you have.

Stop expecting too much

Be more spontaneous because expectations can somewhat alter your direction. It can block you from discovering your talents, so never set the bar too high to the point of your forgetting who you truly are. Once you learn the art of letting go of your expectations, you will see that it is so much easier to be your true self regardless of the situation that you are facing. Examine each of your expectation. Let go of those which you think are disproportionate for you.

Let go of relationships that are by nature, conditional

At this point, let go of other people's expectations. Stop busying yourself with living another person's life by following what others are saying. Unconditional relationships are meant to nurture you with support and not torture you with unreasonable expectations.

Care for yourself and watch your back

Connect with your talents and your true self by doing activities that makes you feel good, fulfilled, and relaxed. It can be any of the following: take a gym class, go to bed early, or read a favorite book. If you have moments of relaxation every once in a while, you will be better oriented to know yourself.

The road towards discovering your true talent begins with knowing yourself from deep within.

Stop Making Excuses

"No excuses and no sob stories. Life is full of excuses if you're looking. I have no time to gripe over misfortune. I don't waste time looking back.

– Junior Seau

Use your gifts, they always say. But there are many of us who keep on believing that we do not have any. If you are stuck with that kind of excuse, there is a great chance that the world will not ever see what you are great at. It is kind of shocking and frustrating finding too many people who dwell on excuses instead of being more proactive.

But we should look at models. There are many successful people around us who could have dwelt on unreasonable excuses. If Zuckerberg, for example, made an excuse that he's just a college undergrad, perhaps we will not have Facebook today. If Obama was overcome by the excuses made by other people for him, then he won't be a two-term US president.

If you will choose to make excuses, you won't discover your gift. Without discovering your inner talent or gift, living life to the fullest will not even be possible. Time is ticking constantly. Before you know it, you might have wasted a lot of time already. Before falling into a situation wherein you no longer have any other option but regret, why not pursue your gifts instead?

Never be afraid of making new discoveries about yourself. It would not entail that much of a threat to the status quo. Many people fall into this absurd belief that discovering your talents would involve making big and radical changes in your life. That is not true. There's no reason for you to think that way.

Here are some steps for you to discover your talents and say no to excuses:

First, you need to open your eyes and wake up to the reality. Give yourself that much-needed wake up call. Whenever you say that you do not have any gifts or talents, just remind yourself that it is not true. Everyone is born with a certain gift or talent that may be unique. It is just that we keep on ignoring our own gifts. Here's what you have to do: keep your heart and mind open. List down what you love to do. Also, take notice of the activities that you find pleasure doing. Think of it this way: talents do not really have to be grandiose, spectacular, or larger-than-life.

Everyone begins with something small. A talent can grow or vanish depending on how you choose nurture it. There are clues that can lead to the eventual discovery of your talents. You can get help from other people. Note that there is a separate chapter meant for discussing how listening to other people's opinions about your skills can lead to the discovery of your talents and gifts.

Aside from other people, listen to the voice from within. You have to trust what your inner self is saying. Listen to your personal intuition and be personally surprised by how accurate your inner voice is. There are other people who call the inner voice a "gut feeling."

Know why you are driven to find your talent. You must have a reason, and you should be very vocal about it. Remind yourself every single day of why you are trying to look for your talent. Are you trying to pursue a higher level of satisfaction? Are you trying to dodge potential sources of pain? Are you trying to relieve some sort of displeasure?

By not making excuses, you will be more open to discoveries. You will know what really motivates you, and at the same time, you will know what kills your spirit.

Try to craft an appropriate response to the question: "What drives you in finding your talent or your gift?" A good response would be, aside from being realistic, is a response that can lift your morale and assist in picking up your momentum. Do you want to experience something better? Do you want to have a higher level of vigor? Would you want to have more enthusiasm? Visualize the answers and firmly set it inside your head. Your answers to these questions will give you an extra push, and it will take you a few steps further each time.

Once you have become aware of your special gifts and talents and the reasons behind each, your mind—both the unconscious and the unconscious—will give you more bits of evidence that will finally cement your firm belief in yourself. Keep on searching, answer the difficult questions including those that are led by "why," and say no to all the excuses that are playing around your head. Never give in to excuses.

Never give in to any of those excuses that are running in your head. It is just a mechanism of your mind to make things easier for you. But these will only hinder your growth as a person and your discovery of your gifts.

Do a Bit of Self-Affirmation

> *"Affirmations are our mental vitamins, providing the supplementary positive thoughts we need to balance the barrage of negative events and thoughts we experience daily."*
> — Tia Walker, The Inspired Caregiver: Finding Joy While Caring for Those You Love

It might be considered as a cliché, but it rings true: you truly are what you think. From an idealists' point of view, the events in our lives are actually deeply rooted from our very thoughts. But from a realist's point of view, life is not only about thoughts. We should do something to translate them into words, and the words should be converted into actions that represent what is inside our head and in our heart.

In finding your true talent and gifts, you need to be careful in choosing your words. You need to choose to say only the things that will be working towards your personal benefit. This way, you will be able to cultivate and nourish your highest personal good. This can be done by doing self-affirmations. They can be very helpful in the process of purification of thoughts and in the restructuring the brain dynamics. If you psych yourself that nothing is truly impossible, you can achieve anything. Meaning to say, it will not be impossible for you to discover your inner gifts and your hidden talents.

By virtue of etymology, the word affirmation comes from the Latin word *affirmare*, which means to strengthen or to make steady. So, in the literal sense, affirmation is the process of steadying yourself. Psychologists say that affirmations increase your chance of harnessing your potentials. But how exactly are you going to do the affirmation process?

First, you have to believe that you possess a certain talent, gift, or potential. Then, you have to do the affirmation verbally. Verbalize your ambitions and dreams and say it clearly to yourself. By doing this, you will instantly refuel and empower yourself via reassurance. The wishful thinking—that you will be able to find your talents—can then turn into reality.

Self-improvement and self-discovery can truly occur through self-affirmation. In fact, neuropsychologists have conducted studies that will prove that such affirmations can result to physiological change. In fact, the physiological change occurs in the brain through the process of rewiring. This is very similar to exercise because it can increase the level of hormones that make you feel better about yourself. The effect of such hormones is the upsurge of positivity and happy thoughts transmitted in your neurons. Additionally, it has been established that affirmations are very important in the avoidance of negative speech, negative thoughts and their manifestation, which are negative actions.

In shaping our future, and in the process of knowing ourselves better and unraveling our capabilities, it is always important to master the art of verbalizing our thoughts. Spiritual advisers are very consistent in saying that the universe can be influenced by each word that we utter. The art that we should master is the art of dictating our wishes. Believe it or not, the universe truly responds. Here are some affirmations that prove to be helpful in unraveling your talents:

(*) I am my own life's architect, and I have the capability to strengthen its foundation and select the contents.

(*) The energy that I have now is overflowing, and it translates to true joy.

(*) I am perfectly happy. I have a brilliant mind. I have a tranquil spirit.

(*) No amount of negative thoughts or low points can put me down.

(*) I have endless talents. I will begin using them all today.

(*) Those who harmed me in the past, I forgive them all now. I detach from them and the pains they caused me peacefully.

(*) I have a lot of compassion from deep within, and it will not allow me to dwell on anger again because I have a lot of love to give.

(*) I have what it takes to be truly successful.

(*) My endeavors are all leading to success.

(*) My mind is brimming with creative ideas.

(*) I choose to be happy because I have a lot of blessings and accomplishments.

(*) I have the unlimited capability to overcome any challenge. My chance to being successful someday is infinite.

(*) I choose to stand by my decisions because they will help me succeed.

(*) I will prosper because I choose to be positive. Life has a lot more to offer.

(*) I choose to detach myself from negative habits and create new and positive ones.

(*) Many people know that I am worthy of their respect and admiration.

(*) I have a family that supports me every step of the way and my friends are equally wonderful.

(*) I have a high level of confidence because I know what I am truly worth.

(*) The things that I am dealing with now are mere preparation for something that is really good.

(*) No one can destroy me. No amount of distractions can break me.

(*) Pain is temporary, glory is forever.

(*) I plan today to have the perfect kind of tomorrow.

(*) The universe will allow me to find my true talents. My dreams will soon become a reality.

(*) I was born to be a great person. No obstacles or difficulty can stop me.

(*) I always function with a clear mind. I decide with a pure heart.

(*) All my fears and hesitations are slowly but surely disappearing.

These affirmations can be utilized in order to find your strengths and locate your talents and gifts. With these, you will better communicate with the universe and invite positive energy. Dreams and aspirations do become a reality.

Listen to Others

"This is the problem with dealing with someone who is actually a good listener. They don't jump in on your sentences, saving you from actually finishing them, or talk over you, allowing what you do manage to get out to be lost or altered in transit. Instead, they wait, so you have to keep going."

— Sarah Dessen, Just Listen

Listening, in itself, is a gift. Not everyone gets to master it because not everyone realizes its true worth. But if you can be a great listener, you will have a better idea of what's really happening around you. You will also see yourself in a much better light if you will listen to what other people are saying.

If you aspire to find your true talent and aspirations, you need to find a good leader, coach, and facilitator. And you should listen to what they have to say.

If you will choose to listen, you will build that sense of trust. Other people will trust you and your talent, and you will begin to trust in yourself if you will learn how to listen. In the process of listening to what others have to say, you can change your perspective and decide to make things a bit better.

If you learn how to listen, you will find out other people's justification behind the talents, skills, and gifts that they see in you. Also, the more you listen sincerely, the more credible you will appear to be. If you are credible, it will be much easier for them to believe in your skills and talents. It will be easier for you to reach your dreams.

Furthermore, if you will learn how to listen properly, you will find out that there are people who can appreciate your worth. By showing that you know how to listen, other people will show a greater degree of support and concern to you. In the process of listening, you will not only discover your talent, you will also show people that you respect them and that they are important to you.

In addition, listening can help you get things and tasks done. By actively listening, you can better identify and set goals.

By listening, you can acquire all sorts of information. Note however, that some of the information that you will acquire may not be among those that you need. Some are very useful while some are worth keeping. Either way, keep your ears, mind, and heart open.

Finally, listening helps open the idea of exchange. If you are in the process of unraveling your talent, then listen on how you can further improve what you already have. This way, you will be a step closer to your goals.

Keep your ears, heart, and mind open. You will be surprised by how much you will learn about yourself and your talent by simply listening.

Understand and Practice the Art of Solitude

"We must become so alone, so utterly alone, that we withdraw into our innermost self. It is a way of bitter suffering. But then our solitude is overcome, we are no longer alone, for we find that our innermost self is the spirit, that it is God, the indivisible. And suddenly we find ourselves in the midst of the world, yet undisturbed by its multiplicity, for our innermost soul we know ourselves to be one with all being."

— Hermann Hesse

Having some time alone is essential in the process of self-discovery because it helps you in better connecting with your inner self.

Experts say that if you want to know your talent, you need to spend a significant amount of your time alone. But the sad thing is that solitude can now be truly considered as among the lost arts. Truth be told, solitude is usually correlated with antisocial tendency of individuals. People who dwell in antisocial behaviors are oftentimes misjudged as being soaked in sadness and loneliness.

But don't fall into such hasty generalizations. Solitude cannot be equated to sadness. Instead, it is a healthy mechanism wherein you can derive quite a number of psychological and physical benefits.

So, what exactly are the benefits of solitude?

Solitude gives you the chance to relax a bit and have a fresher line of thought; you can better unwind with the help of solitude because the brain will be able to take a good rest and replenish itself. Not having any companion around means that you have no distractions to deal with and you can clear your thoughts. That way, you can better think and focus.

Solitude helps in uncovering your talent because it improves productivity and increases the level of concentration. By concentrating well, all of the interruptions and distractions will be effectively removed. You can now focus on your quest to find out what sort of talent or gift lies within.

Solitude gives you the chance to hear your inner voice and better discover yourself. If you are always with other people, you will tend to neglect what you truly want to say. Your opinion will most likely be ignored, and your desires will not be considered really important. Other people's voices tend to "drown" your inner voice. Never let that happen. Try solitude.

Solitude buys you the much needed time to do an in-depth thinking. The things that you have to do on a day-to-day basis seem to have no ending. In order to momentarily free yourself from such, you must first take some time alone to think of things that are important to you. That way, you will be able to enhance your creativity.

Solitude is beneficial because it enhances your skill in solving problems in a more effective manner. By taking some time alone, you will be able to free yourself from distractions.

Your relationship with other people is more likely to be enhanced if you experience solitude every once in a while. If you spend some time with yourself on a regular basis, you can better understand what you want to achieve and what sort of dreams you wish to realize someday. Solitude also helps you make choices that are better aligned with your goals. You can better appreciate the talents that you already have if you are experiencing solitude.

In case you are wondering how exactly you can spend time in solitude, here are some techniques that you might find useful.

Disconnect with the world

Solitude can be a bit challenging to achieve because of the prevalence of gadgets and other forms of technology. So in order to do this effectively, disconnect. Turn off your Android phone and disconnect from the Internet. Unplug your television.

Go to the workplace one to two hours earlier than the usual

That way, you can be sure that there is no one yet in the workplace. You can buy time for yourself to meditate and spend some quiet time alone.

Do not leave your room and lock your door

This is the simplest option that you can take. No need to go somewhere far away. Just lock the door, put a sign and make the world understand that you are spending this time alone.

Try to eat your lunch alone

As a rule, never eat at your work desk. While it is a good time to catch up with friends, it is an equally good opportunity for you to catch up with yourself. You do not have to eat your lunch alone every single day. Doing this option at least once a week is more than enough.

Put the "me time" on schedule

If you are keeping a planner, make sure that you literally mark the date for the scheduled solitude so that you can spend time discovering your talents and potentials. Just like any other activity, if you are not going to put it on schedule, you will have this tendency of leaving it out.

Spending some time alone is perfect for knowing what lies within your mind and heart. It is also good

for uncovering your hidden talents. Solitude is definitely not for the lonely. It is for the curious.

Recognize and Develop Your Talent

> *"There is a fountain of youth: it is your mind, your talents, the creativity you bring to your life and the lives of people you love. When you learn to tap this source, you will truly have defeated age."*
>
> *– Sophia Loren*

You are probably aware of your basic skills. More than anyone else, you can tell what you can and what you cannot do. And these basic skills are usually the starting point of truly extraordinary talents. But it begins with recognizing the existence of the skill so that you can do something to develop and work on it further.

Many people do not get to maximize their skills and reach the full realization of their talents because they chose to ignore what they already have. For example, if you are sensitive to melodies and tunes, do not ignore your skill and capabilities connected to it. Try to sing more. Join a choir. Select a voice coach who can monitor your progress. A lot of talents have been lost because of the owners' decisions to ignore what they have.

Time and again, it has been proven that it is always easier to recognize other people's talents and ignore your own. We often compare what we have to what others have, but that should not be the case. You are unique and your skill set is never identical with that of others. There might be some sort of resemblance, but no two skill sets and talents are identical.

It all begins with discovering and recognizing your talent. Be sure to search your personal, artistic, and creative abilities. Enumerate the activities that you wish to be engaged in. By making this list, you will be able to point out your talents and you can begin enhancing them.

The next step is doing something to actively develop your talent. Talents take a great deal of effort and time to develop, so you should be serious about this feat. If you can remember the time when you are trying to learn walking, writing, and reading, it can be as tedious as that. Others compare developing an existing talent with learning a new language. It takes some serious and conscious effort. You should recognize the fact that perhaps you need to spend some time practicing and rehearsing.

Of course it can be tedious, tiring, and exhausting. A lot of people have already given up on developing or honing their talents. They end up regretting that they did not pursue their talents because they found themselves in a situation wherein they needed it.

On the other hand, there are a lot of people who are thankful for honing their talents in the past despite the difficulty they faced in the past. It pays off to discover, recognize, and develop your talent.

Talents are very much like problems. Unless you recognize their existence, you won't be able to do something about it.

Believe in What You Can Do

"Believe in yourself, and the rest will fall into place. Have faith in your own abilities, work hard, and there is nothing you cannot accomplish."

– Brad Henry

You are a unique being. As a special individual, you need to recognize the fact that the world will not be complete unless you share your talent and capability. Believe in your potentials and in what you can actually do. Never say "I can't" because it can only invite negativity. Whenever you feel bad, ask people who care and those who are ready to provide you with the necessary support.

If you feel that you cannot do it anymore, just tell yourself: "This too shall pass." Whenever you feel like saying: "I've reached my limit," just remember that your potentials are limitless. Aspire to either maintain or improve. Just do not stop. Strive to be better every single time.

Again, it is important to listen to criticisms and take them constructively. Of course, not all opinions about you and your talent will be positive. Sometimes, they can be disheartening if you will take them the wrong way. No matter what other people say, try to aspire for improvement. That is the only way to go. Never lose your passion and face the challenges with courage.

Finally, you need to learn all the necessary skills to make your talent extraordinary. Study what it takes to be better and to develop your talent. You may read several resource materials like books. Also, you can ask people who are willing to be your critic or mentor. Watch movies and take lessons that will enhance your world view. Never be afraid to do your best.

If ever you make mistakes, never give up. The mistakes will only teach you and assist you in making your talents better.

Believe in your talent. Be the first to have faith. And never give up. Strive to be the best.

Give Everything Else a Try

"All growth is a leap in the dark, a spontaneous unpremeditated act without benefit of experience."

– Henry Miller

Be a natural. Never be afraid to spontaneously show your talents. Feel free to sing, dance, play any instrument, paint, rap, or act. Keep your hand full—literally and figuratively. If you can play any sport—be it indoor or outdoor—do not hesitate to play. Do what you can do with one hundred percent passion.

You may find yourself to be a mediocre in things that you do for the first time, but there are only a handful who can do thing perfectly in their first try. Give every single talent a try because it is the only way that you can discover what you can do and what you cannot do. Keep a journal or a record to take note of the things that you can be potentially good in. Take note of the ones that you are comfortable doing. If you are not good in something, be extra honest to admit it so that you will not be wasting time doing it.

In a lot of instances in our life, we tend to tell ourselves that we can't do something. Technically, it is alright to come up with such a conclusion if you have already tried. But the biggest mistake here is if you give up even without trying. It is analogous to putting up that white flag even before you meet your actual enemy.

Be open to surprises. The best times in a person's life are usually when he or she surprises themselves. Once you experience this, you will find something interesting in yourself again.

If you haven't tried rock climbing yet, try it. If you have not tried scuba diving, give it a go. If you haven't tried writing a book, ask someone who can. Put up a business. Start small.

Never be afraid to fail. Even failures present important lessons.

It might be helpful to take into consideration the things that you already know. What are your skills? What can you do? From these bits of information, you have a clue on what is the best thing that you should do.

There is no harm in trying. Never give up unless you have already given a good fight.

Step out of Your Comfort Zone

"I want to challenge you today to get out of your comfort zone. You have so much incredible potential on the inside. God has put gifts and talents in you that you probably don't know anything about."

– Joel Osteen

While providing you comfort, the comfort zone can be some sort of labyrinth that can limit what you can do. There are a lot of people who get stuck in their comfort zone and they end up not trying anything new.

By choosing to stay inside your comfort zone, you deny yourself of all forms of changes. You say no to negative changes, but you also forego the positive one. By staying inside that circle of comfort, you do not give yourself a chance to spend some effort and time to aspire for what you dream and aspire for.

Why is this the case then? Simple—because it is uncomfortable to step out of the comfort zone. And you can't blame yourself for being too afraid of the unknown and the uncertain.

Is there a shortcut towards luring yourself out of the comfort zone? There are simple techniques, but these usually take time. Here are some of the steps that you can take:

Mix up the small things and surprise yourself as often as possible

For example, when it comes to music, never stick to a single genre. Try new kinds of music. Download tunes that you haven't tried before. See if you will enjoy it. The same goes with food. Pick something from the menu that you have not tried before. When you buy books, try a title that does not fit your personality well. Finally, when you are going home, try a path that you haven't tried before. By doing these, you will most likely try to develop a talent that you never thought that you have before.

Take it one step at a time

Never rush. Facing changes can be very difficult. It can be scary to make the big shift. The result is to procrastinate. With that, no positive changes can be expected. In order for you to step out of your comfort zone, try to take really small steps towards your goal. You do not have to be in a hurry. Sometimes, it is better to get there slowly.

Never do it alone

It is best to step out of the comfort zone if you know that you are not alone. If you have a friend who also wishes to discover his hidden talents, encourage him to join you in your quest towards self-discovery. It is always easier to go somewhere if you know if you have company.

The comfort zone can only provide you comfort, nothing more and nothing less. If you want to experience something new and exciting in your life, try to step out of it. Your extraordinary skills and talents can only be found if you choose to ignore your comfort for once. It is going to be truly worth it.

Practice and Develop Your Talent

"Use what talents you possess; the woods would be very silent if no birds sang there except those that sang best."

– Henry Van Dyke

Practice is the only key towards perfection. Many basketball superstars once found themselves imperfect or mediocre in their craft. They chose to spend time and effort to practice and develop their skills.

Practice is the only way for you to control your talent. You can only experience progress if you are determined in developing your gift. A lot of skills that are necessary for perfecting a talent require a lot of repetition. Yes, it can take a few hours, several days, numerous weeks, or even years before you can truly say that you are ready to show the world your talent.

For once in our life, we have already shown the pure determination. If you find yourself talking or walking right now, it is because of the fact that you had the determination to learn when you were a toddler. If you can only use that level of determination and will power in every single endeavor that you are involved in, no talent is impossible to perfect.

At the end of the day, do not complain. Just do something to be better, and you will be surprised at the result.

Once you are done with this, you are ready to show the world your talent. When you are ready, never hide it. Pick an audience and sing, dance, or ask them to listen. A talent is worthless unless it is shared. The joy that it can cause others can never be paralleled.

Practice is the only key towards perfection. Never lose that passion. Keep on trying.

How to Apply Key Ideas for the Best Results?

This compendium discusses several techniques for you to discover your talent. Now, it is up to you to put these tips into action.

Your talents will remain hidden unless you do something about it. Show the world what you can do and you will be surprised with the amount of joy that you will be able to share. Not to mention the happiness that you will feel due to the sense of fulfillment.

How To Learn Any Language Fast

Have you been planning to learn a new language? What are your reasons for learning the new language? Is it because you plan to visit another country and want to know a few words/sentences that will ensure you are not clueless during your visit? Or do you simply want to learn another language for the sake of it? Well, whatever your reasons are for learning another language, it is important that you are fully prepared as you commence your learning process because learning another language, especially as an adult, is not easy. But this shouldn't scare you because you can learn another language by acquiring the right set of skills.

This book will help you to acquire the needed skills that will enable you to learn a new language, find the correct tools to study the language, find the best way to study and stay motivated as you learn the new language. It will cover areas such as how to learn grammar, pronunciation, and vocabulary.

Getting Started

"If you talk to a man in a language he understands, that goes to his head. If you talk to him in his own language, that goes to his heart"

- Nelson Mandela

Did you know that with all the English words available for use, English speakers only utilize 300 words sixty-five percent of the time in their written materials? This means that anyone who knows just over three hundred words can make decent conversation and can be able to understand more than half of what is written. This is also true of other languages. Think about it. What do you talk about day in day out? You will obviously find that in your day-to-day life, there are recurring conversations. You talk about your work, what you are going to eat, where you want to go, your hobbies, your friends, your goals, travelling, your family and anything else that may interest you. There are certain words (vocabulary) that are associated with the conversations you have each day. Your goal should be to learn those words first and fast. You can do this by following some basic principles. These are:

Set realistic goals

Goals are important in life. However, sometimes enthusiasm makes individuals set unrealistic goals that they cannot achieve not because they are unable to, but because their timing is off. The trick to setting goals is to have a big goal and several smaller goals that will help you to achieve that bigger goal. For example, if you want to learn three hundred words within a month, you have to learn just ten words each day for thirty days. Add on to the words each day and use them in sentences. This way, you will continue to build up on your vocabulary.

Develop a language habit

One secret to quickly learning a new language is to develop a language habit. When you habitually use the words you are learning, you are not likely to forget them anytime soon. Repetition is the key to recollection. This means that you need to incorporate the language in your life. Begin by labeling items around the house. This way, whenever you see the items, you will see the name and the names will begin to stick in your mind. You should also get children's books to read because these come with many images and illustrations. Another way to turn language learning into a lifestyle is to use technology. You can change the settings on your phone and your computer to the language you are learning. This will force you to learn new vocabulary fast as you try to figure out what name means what.

Stop worrying about mistakes

Many people, even those who already know some new vocabulary, hesitate to converse with others because they fear making mistakes. Unfortunately, not conversing slows down the learning process. On the other hand, conversing with others who know the language you are trying to learn will enable you to make rapid progress. This is because you will have the chance to articulate the words, learn good pronunciation and learn other words due to the communication. Any mistakes you make will be an added opportunity to learn not only how to use the proper words but also how to use other words.

Key point/action step

Stop worrying about how you will sound to others. Instead, focus on achieving your language goals and improving yourself day by day.

Materials And Tools You Need To Study A New Language

"Learn everything you can, anytime you can, from anyone you can; there will always come a time when you will be grateful you did."

- Sarah Caldwell

In order to learn any new language fast, you need to equip yourself with the right materials and tools. Fortunately, in this age of technology, there are various possibilities to choose from. These are:

Dictionaries

A dictionary is an important tool to have when you are learning another language. This is because dictionaries come not only with words but also with meanings. As a learner, you may want to try out the bilingual dictionary. This way, you will be able to search for the meaning of the words in both languages for easier understanding. A pocket dictionary is best for when you are outside the house as it allows you to quickly refer to it whenever you think of a word you want to check out. However, it is also best to have a larger dictionary as it will give you more definitions. As you advance in the learning, you may also want to have a monolingual dictionary that will allow you to check for meanings without having to see the translation. This will enhance your learning process.

Phrase books

Communication often happens through the use of phrases. The more phrases you know, the better equipped you will be at language proficiency. It would certainly help to know common phrases as soon as possible. Phrase books are thus quite useful especially if they come with recordings of phrases. This way, you can repeat the phrases aloud until you memorize them and their meanings. You can learn how to pronounce the phrases properly by using the recordings.

Notebook and pen

Even in this world of technology, few things beat a notebook and a pen when it comes to learning a new language. There is just something about manually writing down words and phrases that make them stick in your mind. When you have a pen and paper handy, you can proceed to write down your thoughts in the language you are learning. Later on, you can use the dictionary to ensure that you got the spellings right. You can also note down words as they come into your mind. It would be best to carry your notebook and pen around just in case you have the chance of using them when you take a break from work or school.

Flash cards

Flash cards are definitely resourceful materials. They can help you learn words, phrases, and sentences within a very short time. They can also help you learn definitions and translations while you're at it. You can purchase readymade flash cards if you like but perhaps it would be better to make your own, as this will require some effort on your part. As you write down the words and phrases on one side and their translations or definitions on the other side, you are in effect learning the words. Using flash cards will speed up your learning process.

Language courses

When you are trying to learn a new language, it may be wise to engage in a language course. Language courses are specifically designed to help individuals learn a language. They usually introduce a word or phrase; explain what it means and how it can be used and how to pronounce the words. Language courses also provide examples of sentences using the words and give learners some exercises to ensure that they have understood the given words. Courses with textbooks and accompanying cassettes or CDs are more useful as you can not only read the words but also hear how they are pronounced.

Audio devices

Audio devices are great for learning languages. This is because you can continue listening to them even as you go about your day. When you hear the words spoken aloud, you learn how the words are pronounced and they start becoming familiar to you. Audio courses go a step further to provide dialogues, instructions, and exercises. The words and their meanings are well explained. Words that have different meanings or that look similar but are pronounced differently are also brought to your attention.

YouTube

I think it is important that I mention this one individually because it is what will teach you more things than anything else will especially if you want to practice alone before putting your skills to practice when you start talking to people actively. There are countless lessons on literally every language around the world so you can be sure that you won't be short of language instructors. As you search for lessons, it is always important to look for those taught by native speakers of the language because these will help you pronounce words correctly. Don't rely on online translators like Google Translator to learn any language because the system is really flawed. The automated translators don't get the pronunciations right many of the times, which means that you might end up with some funny accent that will only serve to embarrass you.

Skype

If you cannot find someone to talk to when learning a foreign language, Skype is always a click away. You can try to find native speakers of the language then talk to them on Skype just to improve your pronunciation on that particular language. If you are looking for people to speak to, you can always find them on many of the freelancing platforms like Guru.com, Upwork.com (former oDesk), Elance.com, Freelancer.com etc; the options are limitless. Don't be afraid to talk to strangers; you will actually discover that some of them are happy to have a friend in another country!

Key point/action step

Take every opportunity to learn your language of choice. Learning does not only occur in the classroom but it can be achieved by observing and learning from what's around us.

How To Create Time To Learn A New Language

"The limits of my language are the limits of my world."

- Ludwig Wittgenstein

Although human beings appreciate the value that learning new things can bring into their lives, they often find themselves struggling when it comes to accomplishing their goals. There is never enough time to do other things so that one can embark on learning a new thing. The same can be said about learning a language. You may be determined to learn a new language but that doesn't mean that other aspects of your life cease to exist. Instead of giving up on your endeavor, you should:

Schedule time

If you are waiting for free time to begin your language studies, stop waiting. There's never enough time in the world to cover everything you might want to do. At the end of the day, you might find yourself wondering 'where time went' simply because you did not schedule study time. You must make a conscious effort to include language study in your schedule. This means you have to prioritize your day to ensure that you have enough time to practice your language skills. You don't have to schedule long hours of learning. You can divide the study time into smaller/shorter periods throughout the day.

Multitask

Multitasking is an important skill to acquire when you want to cover several things at the same time. Many activities such as doing household chores, exercise, and gardening can be done with other activities such as studying or language practice. Of course, the activity will determine the type of language skill you practice. For example, if you are jogging, you can listen to songs in another language but it would be very difficult to practice writing while you are jogging. Try to find activities that can blend with your listening skills, writing skills and speaking skills. This way, you will be able to practice different sets of skills even as you do other activities.

Listen to radio stations

One way to quickly grasp another language is to listen to a radio station in that language. Radio stations have various radio shows. They play songs and have radio presenters conversing with listeners and reading news. They have advertisements and announcements. All these situations use language. As you listen to a presenter talk or a song playing, your ears begin to tune into the sounds and rhythms of the language you are learning. Even when you don't fully understand the meaning of the words, you become attuned to how they sound. You also learn how to grasp the gist of the conversation by recognizing the words surrounding words you don't know yet.

Use flashcards

Flashcards are easy to use and you can carry them with you as you go about your day. You can have several flashcards for the day and ensure that you study them whenever you get some time. The advantageous thing about using flashcards is that you can whip them out whenever you want to check something and then put them away again.

Key point/action step

Don't wait for time to find you. Instead, go out of your way to create time.

The Best Way To Study A Language

"Learning another language is not only learning different words for the same things, but learning another way to think about things."

- Flora Lewis

Studying a language should be done in such a way that learning will not become burdensome. Learning new things is often exciting but challenging, hence, you need to find the right balance if you intend to learn a new language fast. You should:

Make a study schedule

It's not enough to decide that you are going to learn a new language. You need to make a study schedule that will detail when you are going to study and what you are going to cover. Your schedule should encourage not only language learning but also retention. This means that you should study frequently. Plan to learn a few minutes each day rather than spend one day each week trying to learn everything you can. Studying in small portions more frequently will enable you to learn the language faster.

Learn the basics first

It is important that you first learn the basics. A good foundation will set the tone for the rest of your language learning experience. Things such as orthography and pronunciation may take some time to master but they are what you will base your language learning skills upon.

Allocate adequate time

Once thing you should know about language learning is that some things will be easier to learn than others will. You may find yourself grasping some things quickly but when the going gets tough, you may become discouraged. Don't be disheartened if you find yourself not learning as fast as you had envisioned. Instead, revisit earlier language lessons before tackling fresh lessons as this will help you to strengthen your learning foundation.

Set targets

Targets exist for a reason. They make language learning more interesting and challenging. As you learn a new language, you will be motivated to reach a certain target you have set. However, it is important to set the right target since setting an achievable target will work towards alleviating boredom and encouraging you to reach your target, but if you set a target that is too high, you may become discouraged.

Accept mistakes

Mistakes come with language learning. However, some learners are so worried about making mistakes that the fear hampers their learning. As you start learning a language, your main goal should be to communicate in such a way that you get your message across. Things such as using the correct tenses and inflexions will come later as you become more fluent in the language. Treat mistakes as a chance of learning and not as an obstacle.

Revise the lessons

It is easy to think that you have mastered a lesson immediately after you have learned it. This is because the words and phrases are still fresh in your mind. However, without revising what you have already learnt, you will have difficulty recalling the lessons. Thus, you should endeavor to revise your lessons as often as possible. You can go over the lessons a day after you have done them and then revisit them again after a few days and then after a few weeks.

Enjoy yourself

When you're having fun, learning becomes easier. This is because your brain will associate it with a pleasant activity and you will be able to retain more than you would have if you were always serious. Include things such as games, tongue twisters, songs, and jokes in your language learning. The games you include should become more challenging as your language skills grow.

Combine language learning with your interests

Once you start to grasp the new language, you need to incorporate it in the things that are dear to you.

Key point/action step

In order to learn a language fast, you need to plan and put your plan into action. Set smaller goals that will enable you to achieve greater goals and you will be okay if you follow your plan.

Learning Pronunciation

"Quote A special kind of beauty exists which is born in language, of language, and for language."

- Gaston Bachelard

An important part of learning a new language is learning its pronunciation. Pronunciation can change the meaning of words and affect how people connect to you. There are various ways you can learn to tune your ear to the sounds and rhythms of a language.

Learn from a native speaker

One way you can learn the proper pronunciation of a new language is to get it right from the source. A native speaker of the language can teach you how to enunciate the words well. However, you need to ask the native speaker to speak slowly. This will help you observe the shape of their lips as they make the sounds. You should mimic the native speaker to ensure you get the pronunciation right.

Listen to recordings

Many language courses come with guides and exercises on pronunciation. This means that all you have to do is to listen carefully and let the information sink in. The good thing about recordings is that you can listen to them when you are almost anywhere. You can also listen to them as you engage in other activities. You need to ensure that you don't engage in passive listening. Instead, try out the pronunciations as you listen to them.

Listen to songs

Songs are big on rhythm and enunciation. They also sound nice and thus can make listening to them fun. Listening to songs in a new language will help your pronunciation. You should have a copy of the lyrics written out. This way as the song plays, you can check out the words against the pronunciation.

Listen to an audio book

Another way to tune your ears to pronunciation is by listening to audio books. Technology has made it easier to have both audio books and written books. This means your learning will be easier if you could have the two together. This way, you will be able to listen to the audio and then use the written book to follow through as the audio plays or whenever you want to check out a word.

Listen to the radio or watch a television show

You can listen to practically any radio station around the world due to the presence of online radio stations. You just have to find the right station and the right radio show. This means you have to do some little digging but fortunately, most radio stations have a program lineup that makes it easier to identify suitable programs. Once you decide on the station and the show you will be listening to, find out more about the show and what the show generally talks about. It helps when you listen to radio shows even when you do not understand the words. Over time, you will be able to note down things such as sentences, questions, pauses, and inflexions. The words will also become recognizable to you.

Television shows are another way to boost your pronunciation. Do your research so that you don't fail to understand anything when you are watching the shows. For example, if you are watching a sports show, do some research on the common vocabulary used for sport terms. This way, when you hear the words, you will have an idea of what the conversation is about. Become an active participant by noting down important points of what the show is talking about. As you follow the conversation, you will begin to identify sentence boundaries and various words. Of course, you need to make sure that you don't overdo it. Take breaks whenever necessary. After all, you can always listen or watch the shows the next day.

Key point/action step

Pronunciation is part of language. The sooner you learn it, the better.

Learning Vocabulary

"Americans who travel abroad for the first time are often shocked to discover that, despite all the progress that has been made in the last 30 years, many foreign people still speak in foreign languages"

- Dave Barry

Vocabulary makes up a language. If you are able to identify the different types of words and make sense of them in a sentence, then you can confidently communicate in another language. However, in order to learn vocabulary fast, you need to keep in mind some things. These are:

Seek out familiar words

Languages often borrow from one another. This means whatever language you are trying to learn has words and meanings that are similar to your native language; it would help you a lot to learn what those words are and become familiar with them. Additionally, you should learn to associate words with familiar mental images. This way, you will be able to recall their meanings with little difficulty. This tactic is especially useful with words that may prove difficult to remember. You can draw an image or associate a difficult word with a word that sounds similar to it in your native language.

Learn in blocks

Words usually come connected or related to other words. For example, a simple word such as 'spoon' comes related to other words such as plates, cups, kitchen, saucers, or utensils in general. You can also use the words clean, dirty, small, and large when describing a spoon. There are also different kinds of spoons. All these words are connected and it would be better to learn them together. This way, you can learn how to say 'a large spoon' as you learn the word for spoon. It is also important to learn words in their proper context. Context is important as it can and does change the meaning of words.

Get the genders right

Gender is part of the human society. And when it comes to language, different genders use different words. It is up to you to know which words should be used with which gender. Write these words down and practice associating them with their appropriate genders. Also, keep in mind that some cultures go further to not only differentiate between genders but also between age groups. For example, you can find a culture that has different greetings for males and females or for young people and older people. It is appropriate that you learn these differences so as not to unknowingly upset native speakers.

Revise the lessons

As you learn a new language, it is important to keep on revising the lessons you have already covered. Create a schedule for doing your revision. You should endeavor to vary the length of time that elapses between revisions. For example, you can revise a lesson after a day, a week, and then a month. This way, the work will keep being fresh in your mind.

Read a lot

Reading improves your vocabulary. The more you read, the more you meet similar words and are introduced to new words. Reading introduces you to synonyms and descriptive words. It enables you to take note of sentence structures and even practice pronunciation. You should therefore endeavor to read as much as you can. As you read, try to figure out what some words mean and see whether you can get the meaning of the sentence. You can also determine whether your guess as to what a word means is correct by searching for its meaning in a dictionary.

Key point/action step

The more words you learn, the better you will be at speaking a language. However, start learning the words that you will need to use in your day-to-day life first before proceeding to other words.

Learning Grammar

"Language is the blood of the soul into which thoughts run and out of which they grow."

- Oliver Wendell Holmes

Learning the proper pronunciation and acquiring a rich vocabulary enables you to communicate using phrases and sentences you have learnt. However, you need to learn grammar in order to construct your own sentences. Grammar involves knowing a variety of things such as:

The word order of sentences

Every sentence has a word order. This word order details where to place the subject, the verb, and the object of the sentence. Unfortunately, not all languages follow the same word order. This means it is important to learn about the word order of the language you are learning. Once you learn the word order, you can begin to construct your own sentences. You can start by arranging a sentence in your native language into the subject, verb, and object. Then arrange the sentence in the language you are learning in order to see what word order it follows. Work with several sentences to get it right and ensure that the translations are correct.

Words changing their shape

Most languages have words that shape shift or change whenever they play certain roles. Nouns, verbs, and adjectives are some of the words you can expect to shape shift. These words can change to accommodate the person performing the action, the number of people involved and the time the action is taking place (tense). It is therefore necessary to note down such distinctions when you are talking about an action. For example, you can say 'she is playing' to indicate that a girl is currently playing outside. However depending on other factors such as time and place, you can change the sentence to 'she played', 'she was playing', and 'she had been playing'.

Look out for gender

Different languages tend to assign genders to nouns. In English, gender is associated with sex and takes on words such as 'he', 'she' and 'it' among others. In some languages like French and Italian, it is easier to identify gendered words because they take on a different spelling. Gender will affect grammar and therefore it is important that you learn the genders represented in the language you are learning.

Identify regular and irregular patterns

One aspect of learning grammar is learning how to identify regular and irregular grammatical patterns. Start with learning the regular patterns before embarking on learning irregular patterns. Keep in mind that verbs that are used commonly are the ones that often have irregular patterns. Therefore, knowing such verbs will make your work easier. Unfortunately, there is no easy way to learn the patterns. You need to put in the work. The more you learn, the easier your work will become.

Key point/action step

Learning grammar will free you. It will enable you to form your own sentences and explore new possibilities.

How To Stay Motivated

"Language is the road map of a culture. It tells you where its people come from and where they are going"

- Rita Mae Brown

Motivation is the key that will enable you to learn a new language. When you are not motivated, you lose interest in whatever you are doing and this will hamper your progress. Various things can cause you to lose your motivation. If the lesson is too hard, you will easily become frustrated. If it is too boring, you will lose interest. On the other hand, if it is too easy, you will have nothing to look forward to. However, there are some things you can do to stay motivated. These are:

Vary your language learning activities

A great way to stay motivated is to vary your language learning activities and work to master different language skills. Find fun and challenging activities to engage in but be patient as you try out new activities as they may take time to get used to. You need to practice your listening skills, reading skills, pronunciation, conversational skills and writing skills. Find fun activities that can test out the different language learning skills and ensure that you vary such activities to prevent boredom.

Have clear goals

If your wish is to learn a new language, you must determine what you want to accomplish or your wish will not turn into reality. It is important to set goals that are achievable, measurable and time bound. Goals like that will keep you on your toes, as you will be working hard to achieve them within the designated period. Instead of generalizing about learning a language, you should have clearly spelt out goals. For example, you can decide to read one book each month as part of practicing your reading skills. You should not only state your goal but also how you plan to achieve it. This way, you will take the necessary steps that will lead you to achieving your goals.

Join a language learning community

Learning something new can turn into an unpleasant chore if you don't have the needed support. Language learning takes time, effort, and patience. It would be easier for you to learn a language if you are part of a language learning community. However, if you are unable to find a group of friends or like-minded people at your local area, you can seek out online learning communities. Find a community that has the same goals as you and that is active. Become an active participant in the community to benefit from it. You should not leave community participation to chance. Instead, schedule your time well and state specifically from what time you will be engaging with the community. A community will help you to stay motivated as you become proficient in the language you are learning.

Immerse yourself

Many people marvel when little children seem to grasp a language faster than adults do. The truth is that when children learn a language, they don't have the luxury of comparing it with their native language. They learn the new language as it is, without making comparisons, and that is how you should strive to learn a new language. This means that you should not be overly concerned with translations. Instead of constantly searching for the meaning of words in a dictionary, you should use images and illustrations to understand what the words mean. This is part of language immersion.

When you immerse yourself, you engage in activities that embrace not only the language but also the culture of the native speakers. This means you should speak in your language of choice, engage in various activities that make use of the language (theatre, movies, sports, festivities) and learn how to incorporate the language in all you do (changing your phone settings and computer language).

Key point/action step

Find various ways to motivate yourself in order not to lose interest in learning a new language.

How to Apply What You've Learned?

After learning about how you can learn a new language fast, you need to take active steps in order to start on your journey. Begin by deciding which language you are going to learn and familiarizing yourself with speakers of those languages. A map will come in handy and you can read guides about the country that speaks that language. Knowing the history of a people can whet your interest and enable you to immerse yourself in their language and culture. You should then get the learning materials you will require and schedule time for doing your learning. Keep yourself motivated by engaging in different learning activities and by including suitable games in your language learning. And lastly, use every opportunity to learn and speak your language of choice.

How To Learn Any Skill Fast

Think about all the things in life you've always wanted to do. Learn a language, ride a bike, climb Mount Everest. Everyone has a list of things they want to do and they usually put it in the back of their mental attics and label it 'maybe, someday, when I find the time.' Then after gathering a plethora of things to do, people end up sitting in front of the television or computer idling away their hours. They go about their days like this because deep down they know – or think they know – that they neither have the skill nor time to get these things done; but then again, deep down, they also know that they would like to learn how to.

What usually deters people from going out and learning all that they can is the perceived barriers to learning. They feel that they will be setting themselves up for frustration and failure. Ultimately they see it as a waste of time. This is indeed a reasonable concern. However, what is really gained without a little grit and hard work? Who can ignore the satisfaction of having learned something, from scratch no less? Wouldn't it be cool if you could do what you've always wanted to by learning quickly? Imagine the fun you could be having with a new set of skills.

Well, everyone starts out unskilled. Everyone has to realize this. Even some persons branded as prodigies had to learn skills to make use of or compliment their innate abilities. What everyone needs to know is there are less painful and frustrating ways of achieving what they want in the least time possible.

This book is precisely meant to help you do just that – make learning easier. It is not a 'learn how to....in a day' book, although it is quite possible to learn something in a day. Instead it is a guidebook to help you learn the smart and efficient way. Learning will not be instantaneous. However, it can be done considerably easier. This book is meant to help address two important concerns: time and skill. It will teach you how to manage your precious time so that you can learn skills that are fun and dear to you. Get to ride that bike, converse with people from different parts of the world, conquer that mountain you've always wanted to climb – fast! By simply managing how you think about learning, you can achieve quick results you did not even imagine was possible.

In this book, you will find a step-by-step checklist of principles. Each principle has its own chapter explaining how it will help you acquire skills you've always wanted in the least possible time. These are general principles that can be applied to any endeavor, big or small. By the end of this book, hopefully you will be transformed into a learning genius.

Finding a Project You Love

"The best thing that can happen to a human being is to find a problem, to fall in love with that problem, and to live trying to solve that problem, unless another problem even more lovable appears."

- Karl Popper

The first step to skill acquisition is not a complicated one. You simply have to find something that you love to do. This is an important part of the process because every skill is essentially a solution to a problem. So this means that skill acquisition involves finding a solution to a problem or point of difficulty. When trying to learn a skill, you can then expect to hit a lot of snags that can slow you down or ultimately make you quit. Loving the task at hand will lessen the frustration that comes along with learning a skill and solving problems.

Making mistakes will not sting as much if you enjoy what you're doing. You can just shrug it off and laugh. When you do make gains in learning the skill, it will be all the more satisfying. Ultimately, it will give you the impetus to work through the struggles and apply more effort. More effort and less frustration would translate to acquiring the skill faster.

Finding the suitable skill or activity for you is almost entirely personal. It mostly involves finding a balance between the enjoyment you will get out of the skill and the urgency or need for it. While nothing is wrong with learning a skill just for fun, nothing beats learning a fun skill because you know you can use it. Assess what your interests are and rank them. Now cross-reference this to which skills are useful to you at the moment. It is natural for you to learn higher ranking skills than lower ranking ones.

For example, you think that learning Italian would be cool. If it has been your life-long dream to learn it, then you will most likely learn it faster. Suppose that you've also wanted to learn Swedish and you also plan on taking a trip there in a few months. The added incentive of actually using the skill will give you more drive to learn Swedish faster than Italian. In fact, you might want to set aside the less useful skill for later.

Remember though that your interests and needs might change over time. So what is important and fun to you now can lose its appeal in the middle of the learning process. So you have to really want to learn something if you want to learn it rapidly.

Find a skill/project that you love, enjoy and can use.

Focusing On Your Skill

"Success demands singleness of purpose. You need to be doing fewer things for more effect instead of doing more things with side effects."

- Gary Keller

One pitfall of deciding to acquire skills is trying to do them all at once. The previous chapter touched upon the issue of having a hierarchy of several interests. You would choose one over the other because it appealed to you more. However, what happens when you can't decide which you like best? Most people would attempt to learn several things at once and end up with nothing.

This happens to be one of the problems of the formal education system: students are forced to learn several skills in a limited amount of time. The result is that they have to juggle things around. At the end of the semester or school year, they are left with no actual skills because they could not focus on just one due to the constraints of the system. You on the other hand, are not limited by the same constraints. You are not forced to learn several things at a time. You have the luxury of focusing on one skill at a time– so use it!

Remember that the goal is to acquire a skill in the least amount of time. So it is just logical for you to take things one at a time so that you can learn your desired skill faster. The more time and effort you put into other skills, the less time and effort you have for your desired skill. If you spread yourself too thin between several things, then you will waste too much energy on switching between skills. You will end up frustrated with one thing and move on to another. This will impede your learning and get you nowhere.

Focus is the name of the game if you want to learn really fast. Focused and deliberate effort on one skill will help you absorb information faster. Your brain is indeed capable of processing several things at one time, but if it gets too cluttered you will not gain much progress. You are trying to minimize impediments to learning and maximize your chances of acquiring your skill. If you really want to learn several skills, it would be better for you to pick one and list the rest of them down for now. You can tackle the others in the future, keeping in mind your level of interest and need for them.

Concentrate your effort on one skill at a time.

Setting Your Goals

"A problem well stated is a problem half solved."

- Charles Kettering

The next step in the process is to set your specific personal goal. Your general goal is to learn a skill. Your specific personal goal is what level of skill you want to acquire. You should be clear on what is good enough to you before you start. Otherwise, you would never know if you've accomplished what you set out to do. If you can tell yourself what you want to achieve, then the only problem left for you is achieving it.

You should be clear on what you will be able to do when you are done learning. The more specific you can make your goal, the easier and faster it is for you to reach. With this goal in mind, you can gauge whether or not you are actually getting closer to learning or if you have to use a few more hours of practice.

Defining your personal goal will usually depend on the reason why you want to learn the skill. If you are learning the skill just for kicks, then you should necessarily want to work at it until you lose the frustration and start having fun at it. If you intend to use the skill for something more serious, you should set your minimum level of performance. Once you reach your minimum goals, you can always choose to get better at the skill or you can cross it off the list and find another project to start.

Generally, the more relaxed your specific goal is, the faster you can acquire it. Remember, you are trying to be capable and sufficient as fast as possible; you are not trying to be the greatest master of the skill yet. You can get to that after. Right now you have to start from somewhere.

Another note on the matter would be thinking of your safety. Some skills have a measure of danger attached to them. Make sure you are aware of these dangers and sufficiently prepare for them. Include them in considering your specific goal. You do not want to hurt yourself in the process of learning.

Lastly, your goal will resonate all through the entire process of learning. It might help to write it down in a progress notebook or post it on your wall. This way, you can always refer back to it when in doubt.

Specify your goal – what you want to be able to do.

Breaking Things Down

"The secret of getting ahead is getting started. The secret of getting started is breaking your complex overwhelming tasks into small manageable tasks, and starting on the first one."

- Mark Twain

When you think of skills, you tend to imagine them as a single unit that you have to learn in its entirety. However, most of the things you label as skills usually consist of smaller parts or sub-skills. Take for example the skill of portrait painting. You would think that it is pretty straightforward: you pick up a brush and start painting things and people. In reality however, it entails many processes such as selecting the kind of medium, subject matter, kinds of brush strokes, color blending, and the like.

If you remember, in the second chapter, it was noted that when you try to learn several things at a time, you will most likely not learn anything at all. The same idea applies here. You should break down your desired skill and tackle each part to ensure focused learning. This keeps you from being overwhelmed by the amount of information you have to take in. You don't have to juggle all the parts in your mind. Instead, you can train your attention on what is at hand then move one to another when you are done.

More importantly, this allows you to see which parts of the skill are essential to beginners and which are better suited for experts. If you can isolate the critical portions of the skill, you can make more progress without being burdened by the less essential things. By stripping the learning program of things that are not important for the goal or performance level you set, you can cut down the time it takes for you to acquire your skill. As an added bonus, each segment of the skill you learn gives you the satisfaction of achieving something quicker. You would expect that each sub-skill can be learned faster than the entire skill itself. Enjoy learning each and you will compound the satisfaction of putting them all together.

Now, bring your attention back to the example of portrait painting. Suppose you set your goal as being able to do an accurate self-portrait in black and white based on photograph. Your goal is specific enough and allows you to cut out parts of the skill such as blending colors and painting moving subjects. Instead, you can prioritize learning sub-skills that are more essential to you, like shading and scaling.

Break your skill into sub skills and prioritize.

Finding the Right Tools

"If you ain't got no axe, you can't cut no wood."

- John Eaton

Most skills you want to learn need some tool or other resource for practicing or performance. If you want to try archery, then you would necessarily need a bow and a bunch of arrows, you can't shoot a basketball without a ball, and so on. Before you get to practicing, you need to know what implements are needed. Make a list of what you need now and will need in the future.

The main idea here is accessibility and convenience. You cannot effectively practice if you have to constantly spend time and effort in looking for things you that you could have prepared beforehand.

Take note of things that you already own. Look for what you can buy or borrow. See what your budget covers based on what you want to achieve. You can lose concentration and drive if you keep on thinking of expenses. More importantly, you can lose resources if you do not plan well, and that is not fun at all.

Cover all the bases so it will be smooth sailing when you start practicing. Remember that some skills do not only require tools, but also venues and environments. You need a skating rink if you want to learn ice skating. You also need a quiet place if you want to learn Chinese meditation techniques. Maximize your time spent training and practicing by having all you need at hand. If your skill has an element of hazard to it, then make sure that you take account for this. Find a practice area away from populated areas if necessary.

Know the things you need and prepare them.

Breaking Down the Barricades

" If you always put limit on everything you do, physical or anything else. It will spread into your work and into your life. There are no limits. There are only plateaus, and you must not stay there, you must go beyond them."

- Bruce Lee

Several things can prevent you from effective practice and ultimately learning. These can be physical barriers in the form of lack of tools, misplacement of things and a disorderly workplace. The constant need to borrow what you need can also serve as an impediment. As stated in the previous chapter, you should make sure you have access to what you need when you need it. This saves you the effort and energy. It ultimately makes for smoother practice and faster learning.

You can also be distracted by external factors such as constant phone calls, television, social networking, and the like. Place yourself in an environment suitable for what you intend to do. Minimize unnecessary distractions that can make you lose momentum and take up precious learning time.

Emotional issues can also prevent you from learning effectively. You might be afraid or embarrassed to start working on your project. You may want to learn something, but it might be a bit dangerous or edgy. Make yourself comfortable by getting safety gear or finding assurance that you will not be hurt. If the activity seems awkward, do it with other people to make you comfortable that you are not doing it alone. Or you can always do it in the solitude of a secluded place so you will not fear ridicule while you are still getting the hang of things. Always keep in mind that you are trying to learn something you would love and enjoy. The satisfaction of acquiring a skill will always trump whatever misgivings you have. Have fun with the learning process and don't worry about failure. Laugh and shrug it off. The more relaxed you are in practicing, the easier it is for you to absorb what you are trying to learn.

You cannot always rely on willpower alone to overcome these barriers while you are practicing or training. You need to take care of these before you even start. Rearrange your surroundings to make it easy for you to begin. You cannot spare any time for distractions if you want to acquire your skills fast and effectively.

Remove all the barriers that prevent you from learning.

Making Time

"You will never find time for anything. If you want time, you must make it."

- Charles Buxton

The above quote is dead on when it comes to time. Most people tend to think that they can miraculously 'find time' in a day to practice. The reality is this never happens. If you do not set aside a certain part of your day for practice, then you will tend to waste hours just idling around. If you decide to learn a skill and you want to do it quick, then there is always the necessary trade-off of spending more time on it and less on other things. So this means it's time to cut down on some less important things like television, video games and surfing the net. The previous chapter already warned you about distractions from starting. Removing these unnecessary impediments will also work to eliminate delays in your skill acquisition.

A good tip is to take a notebook and log how you spend your day in hours. Once you do this, you can visualize your day and shuffle things around to make time. You can see where you waste time and where you can save it. Remember that you have twenty-four hours in a day. Eight of these hours are usually spent sleeping, which is important if you want effective retention of information and training. You are left with sixteen hours that you have to allocate between work and spending time with friends and family perhaps.

You should not neglect your responsibilities, of course. The time left from these activities has to be given to your practice and training. If you really want to learn as quickly as possible, then the trick is to allocate bigger blocks of time for practicing. Uninterrupted practice is always best and leads to better results. A good starting point is to allot at least an hour and a half a day for your practice.

It is also recommended that you commit yourself to do at least a total of twenty-four hours of practice. When you hit a snag, you should push on until you reach the target hours or your target goal. If you find that twenty-four hours seem to be too big an investment for your skill, maybe you should reassess if you really want to learn it. You can move on to another one and come back to it later. Pre-committing a definite amount of time will help you through the rough patches of early practice. You can expect that it will be hard at first and will be filled with frustration.

Setting a twenty-four hour goal gives you something to visualize and is helpful in maintaining your drive. You should look at this as an exercise in persistence. You should not let tiny hindrances stop you from doing what you set out to do. Once you hit the target number of hours, you can assess if you achieved your specific goal if you have not done so earlier. From there, you are in the proper position to decide whether you should keep on practicing or if you are ready to acquire a brand new skill.

Dedicate a definite amount of time to practice.

Finding Feedback

" I think it's very important to have a feedback loop, where you're constantly thinking about what you've done and how you could be doing it better. I think that's the single best piece of advice: constantly think about how you could be doing things better and questioning yourself. "

- Elon Musk

Getting feedback means getting information on whether or not you are doing well. Feedback is very important for learning because it is what tells you when progress is being made. Conversely, it also tells you when more work has to be put in. If you are doing well, carry on or do better. When you see that you messed up, make adjustments and try again.

If you want to gain a skill fast, your feedback also needs to return to you fast and accurate. The longer it takes for you to get feedback, the more time it will take for you to learn because it means more time to wait before you can make your adjustments. The time you can practically get feedback will vary greatly depending on the skill you want to learn.

If you are trying your hand at grafting ornamental plants, then you may not know when the graft is successful for a couple of weeks. However, if you want to learn ornamental pruning, you can immediately see the effects of your practice. You can compare diagrams with your work or you can even ask the neighbor or a local gardener if your work looks good. The best kind of feedback is the most immediate.

You can find feedback in several forms depending on your skill desired. You can find trainers, coaches or other experts who can mentor you while you practice. They are excellent sources of tips, tricks and feedback. For instance, a gym trainer can give you real-time feedback on your weightlifting form while you do it. If you prefer to do things solo, then you can also opt to use video capture of yourself practicing to help assess your progress. Part of your preparation in finding the right tools could include finding implements, measuring devices, computer programs or the like that can help you assess your progress. The more sources of feedback you can find and utilize, the faster you can learn your skill.

Remember that feedback has to be accurate as well. You will be wasting time if you kid yourself with biased and unreliable sources of feedback. You will end up with a big ego and no skill to show for it. Be honest with yourself and admit if you are not doing well so you can objectively assess your results.

Establish a fast and reliable feedback system.

Quick, Timed Practices

" What I have achieved by industry and practice, anyone else with tolerable natural gift and ability can also achieve."

- Johann Sebastian Bach

The early parts of practice will usually test your patience. You will probably feel like time is moving very slow and this will make you feel frustrated. Your mind is simply not wired to accurately tell time. This can lead to frustration and the feeling of fatigue even if you've only been practicing for a short period of time. This can make learning hard and near impossible at times.

The best way to remedy this is to time your practice sessions. Get a countdown timer, set it for say twenty to thirty minutes. Once you start the countdown, you need to practice until the time is up. No excuses. This way, you can stop worrying about time moving slowly. All you have to do is focus on practicing.

Let the timer worry about how long you have been at it. Repeat this over and over extending the countdown over time. This simple process will help you get used to practicing over longer periods of time and help you break through frustration and fatigue.

Doing a lot of these timed practice sessions will help you learn faster. You can set up as many as six of these in a day. Doing this will definitely get you great results in a short period of time with less frustration.

Practice in timed intervals and practice often.

Practicing a Lot

"I fear not the man who has practiced 10,000 kicks once, but I fear the man who has practiced one kick 10,000 times"

- Bruce Lee

When you are starting out, you will most likely be thinking that you have to practice perfectly. After all, they do say that 'perfect practice makes perfect'. However, you should remember that you are not trying to be a grandmaster of the skill just yet. Your goal is to learn the skill and be capable at it in the shortest possible time. Bruce Lee may have been a perfectionist. You are not aiming for perfection. Instead, you should take a leaf from his book when it comes to quantity of practice. Practice your kicks ten thousand times before you think of perfection.

The trouble with aiming for perfection at the onset is that it takes too much time even for a master at the skill. You can just imagine how long it will take for a beginner to do something perfectly without any training at all. Add to that the frustration that this can build up if you expect yourself to perform near perfectly when you are just starting. Keep in mind that you are just starting out, it is alright for you to start out awkwardly.

What is important for you now is to start practicing and practicing often. For rapid skill acquisition, quantity of practice trumps quality. The faster and more often you practice, the easier it is for your mind to pick up patterns and apply these to future sessions. Your mind is hardwired to work with repetition. The more you do something, the easier it will be for you to repeat it. Once you are familiar with the motion or activity, it will be simpler for you to make subtle adjustments to achieve your specific performance level goal.

This is not to say that you should not try to achieve good form when you practice, but this is best done after you have gotten in a few sessions to get used to the skill being practiced. The rule is that your first sessions should be focused on doing the activity or getting used to the motions. When you are familiar with it, try achieving or at least approximating your target level of skill. You can then speed up your training.

The more sessions and the faster you can do them, the quicker you will be able to progress. Of course don't forget the system of feedback you established, you cannot learn without knowing if you are actually improving. The bottom line is that you should not kill yourself over perfection when you are starting out. Focus first on getting more sessions in, progress will follow.

Practice and more practice: quantity of practice first, quality is for later.

How to Apply What You've Learned?

The principles given in these chapters are ideally meant to be followed step-by-step and speak mostly of preparation both physically and mentally for the process of learning new skills. They are made as general as possible to accommodate any skill you wish to learn. They may not all fit perfectly with everything you want to learn, but most will be essential to it. To help you apply these guidelines even better, you can take note of the broader ideas being espoused. This way, you can add to and tweak them to suit your needs.

First, we have the *principle of efficiency*. You should always think of how you can achieve better results through spending the least resources. Resources mean your time, effort, energy and even financial resources. Streamline the learning process so that you can get rid of what is unnecessary and focus on what is essential. You have already eliminated the physical and emotional distraction, what else is slowing you down? Is there anything peculiar to your skill that can be tweaked? You have already determined the core sub-skills, which sub-skill will make learning the others easier?

Second, there is the *principle of orderliness*. Take note of ways that you can structure your learning. An orderly process is always friendly to learning. If you plan your learning in such a way that is logical, you can be sure that you will learn much easier and faster. This is not limited to orderly planning either; you can also consider the orderliness of your practice area. Are your tools where they should be? Is your work area clean? Is it affecting your learning? Are you logging your hours in a proper way?

Third, you have the *principle of managing your expectations*. You cannot expect to learn something immediately. Set your expectations reasonably. This is the reason why you set a specific goal as to your level of skill. Do not feel bad if you do not achieve things right away or if things are taking too long.

You can always go back to the checklist and see if there is something else you haven't considered. Or maybe you need to set your expectations higher for the amount of time you want to invest in the skill. Rapid skill acquisition is about setting manageable skill goals.

Fourth, you should *stack the deck*. Part of your preparation should be to make sure you know as much about the skill you want to learn as possible. Learning should start even before you practice. Stack the decks in favor of getting the best possible result. Read books, watch online videos, visit exhibitions. This will make you familiar with the related ideas and concepts. If you do this, then you will lessen the 'I'm new to this' feeling and speed up progress.

Lastly, *have fun with it*! Learning is an enjoyable process. The principles given in the chapters are meant to take away the frustration and grief that comes with learning, but the experience in itself is fulfilling. Many find that frustrations are part of it. They love a challenge and are not afraid to fail. Having this attitude is very helpful in acquiring skills. Learn to love the process as much as the result. Again, you are not trying to kill yourself over a new skill. Be a learning-junkie, it is one step-closer to becoming a learning genius.

www.ingramcontent.com/pod-product-compliance
Lightning Source LLC
Chambersburg PA
CBHW071814200526
45169CB00018B/274